A Church of the Baptized

Overcoming Tension Between the Clergy and the Laity

by
Rémi Parent

Translated by
Stephen W. Arndt

PAULIST PRESS
New York/Mahwah

Copyright © 1987 by Les Edition Paulines, Montreal. English translation ©
1989 by the Missionary Society of St. Paul the Apostle in the State of New York.

All rights reserved. No part of this book may be reproduced or transmitted in any
form or by any means, electronic or mechanical, including photocopying,
recording, or by any information storage and retrieval system without permission in writing from the Publisher.

Library of Congress Cataloging-in-Publication Data

Parent, Rémi, 1936–
    [Eglise de baptisés. English]
    A church of the baptized : overcoming tension between the clergy and the
laity / by Rémi Parent : translated by Stephen W. Arndt.   p.   cm.
    Translation of: Une Eglise de baptisés.
    Bibliography: p.
    ISBN 0-8091-3076-9 : $10.95 (est.)
    1. Church.   2. Catholic Church—Clergy.   3. Laity—Catholic Church.
4. Catholic Church—Doctrines.
BX1746.P26213   1989
262'.1—dc20   89-9247
                                                                       CIP

Published by Paulist Press
997 Macarthur Boulevard
Mahwah, New Jersey 07430

Printed and bound in the
United States of America

Contents

Foreword	....	1
1.	The Dimensions of the Question	7
2.	God	32
3.	(Jesus) Christ	56
4.	Priests	82
5.	The Mass	108
6.	The Church	132
7.	The World	167
Notes	....	199

FOREWORD

I hesitated a long time before embarking upon the writing of this book. Two reasons finally persuaded me to do it.

The first one was decisive. For several years, and in all the places I had been called upon to serve the church, a cry constantly arose. At times close to anger and burdened by impatience, it was most often a cry of heavy hearts frustrated in their most legitimate aspirations. It was a cry of persons and communities who could no longer stand being under tutelage, whose lay condition seems to prevent them from living fully the church to which they nonetheless continue to cling almost desperately. And the answer given to them is ordinarily without promise for the future. It has so little substance that it is itself a cry. Are we forever condemned to this impossible, ultimately paralyzing dialogue, where one of the partners only nourishes the frustration of the other? Will we ever understand the questions attempting to be formulated in the cry of so many lay people? Will we even give this cry a chance to become a question?

A second reason convinced me to take up the pen. The practice of theology has disabused me of many illusions about the answers it claims to provide. But I have also learned that it is not at all shameful to dedicate one's life to trying to pose the right questions or to pose them at the right time. Is there any other way of progressively entering upon the formulation of answers which give life in the waiting, even if they never satisfy forever? Engaged in a task at once impossible and strictly necessary, does the theologian not render a better service when, walking with his

A CHURCH OF THE BAPTIZED

brothers and sisters, he assumes with them the common condition of those who seek the God of Jesus Christ? Whatever the case may be, my small answers to these questions have sufficed for me to decide to say what I think about the present state of clergy/laity relations and about the ways that seem to me to promise a certain future for the church of today.

I thus do not wish to deny the contribution of my previous reflections and, more generally, of all the work to which my profession as a theologian has invited me. But, among my motivations, the numerous ecclesiastical experiences I have had here and there, and all I am able to know about the present state of my church, have weighed more heavily.

This is a hard book for clerics and for clericalism because they arrogate to themselves an unjustified and an intolerable place in the church. On the other hand, I know several priests and bishops whose spirit of service is entirely admirable. They are, furthermore, the first to deplore the narrowness of the present clerical structures and the little room to maneuver which these structures leave them. One can thus condemn clericalism while recognizing the legitimacy of the ordained ministry. Furthermore, I know too well that any criticism is justified only insofar as it springs from the demands of love.

This book already has a relatively long history. A few years ago, when I was preparing a lecture on the church, an intuition was born which had the fragility and the dynamizing power of every intuition: *the particular question of the laity is ill posed; it will thus remain unanswered as long as one does not gain a better idea of its relations with the totality of our contemporary religious mentality.* Without losing its force, this intuition has progressively left the haziness in which it was shrouded; it has taken on enough content to become a true question, being taken up again here and there on the occasion of a course or lecture, in all the places where the church invited me to be church. Then, on the occasion of a research seminar, this question unfolded, opened

2

FOREWORD

up, and became problematic: *the present structure of clergy/laity relations reflects and nourishes all the relations that constitute our religious landscape, from our relationships with God to our relationships with the world.* The first chapter will explain the meaning of what has been affirmed too rapidly here. But what I am presenting today is a problem, nothing more, but nothing less either. It is understood, of course, that a disagreement on a particular point or judgment does not automatically entail a condemnation of the whole problem.

The formulations I have just employed express my objectives and their limits well enough. I only wish to aid in *shifting the question.* Theology is too bent on understanding each reality of the Christian life as if it constituted an autonomous whole. Concerning the laity, for example, all efforts at reflection are aimed at it as something independent in itself, whereas it exists only *in relation* to the clergy. Will we finally stop considering the clergy and *then* the laity, focusing our attention on the one *or* on the other? What uselessly expended efforts! And what frustrations too! The answer never ceases to escape us. But if the answer is so elusive, it is not in virtue of the legitimate complexities of life. It is because the question itself has been ill posed. Our attention has to turn toward the *relations* that are operative between the clergy and the laity. Then, perhaps, certain knots which stifle the life of the church will begin to be untied.

A synod on the laity is now being prepared. Even if this writing project appears well before the announcement of this synod, one can understand the interest I have in this upcoming event. At the moment I write these lines, Rome has sent to the different churches a text entitled *Lineamenta. Vocation and Mission of the Laity in the Church and in the World Twenty Years after the Second Vatican Council.* I confess that I was doubly saddened at the reading of this text. At first, it appeared to me to be of a distressing theological poverty, stitched together with citations from Vatican II but foreign to the noble intentions of the

3

A CHURCH OF THE BAPTIZED

council, thus running the risk of setting the church back decades. Even worse, I was struck above all by its inappropriate abstraction, a sort of intemporality that indulges in exhilarating exhortations and does not even understand the true questions with which lay people are concretely confronted in their real lives and their daily relations with clerics. I know how pretentious these judgments sound. I only hope that the book will show that they are not without foundation.

The formulation of my hypothesis will perhaps have made it clear why I could feel cramped throughout the writing of this book. In fact, I constantly had to assume four constraints.

I am anxious to state the first constraint as clearly as possible, if only for intellectual honesty. In order for the project to be viable, I had to impose limits on myself to which my future readers must now consent. My first objective is to *pose the question* of the laity, shifting it with respect to the way it is usually posed. If I had not believed that that was worth being shown (and may the reader take the time to follow the demonstration), I should not have invested such efforts in the writing of this book. But the reader will suspect that once the logic of the relations to which we are accustomed has been analyzed, once the question has been posed, the immense work of synthesis will remain. Certain ways of seeing one's relation to God, for example, may be judged unacceptable from a Christian point of view, without, for all that, denying the existence of God and the possibility of entering into relation to him. In the same way, one will see that several approaches to the "priesthood of the priests" seem inadmissible to me. But that does not mean that I refuse all place to the presbyterate and the episcopacy in the life of the church. In a single word, one will necessarily be disappointed if, in undertaking the reading of this book, one expects from it the proposal of a Christian anthropology rearticulated in a new and totally coherent way. I am, of course, suggesting trails for the future. Nevertheless, in order not to lose myself in too vast an enterprise, I myself had to consent to not pushing the work of reconstruction too far. I thought it good to indicate these inevitable limits from the beginning.

Of itself, my problem necessarily leads to fields of investigation where I have to work with very limited competence. In effect, it questions our conceptions of God, of Jesus Christ, of the church, etc., without my being able to claim for each point a sufficient maturity of reflection. Above all, I am working in the field of ecclesiology and of the theology of ordained ministry. It is thus from this starting point that I address my questions to specialists in theology, christology, and each of the other domains touched upon. Thus, I constantly had to renew the following conviction: my answers may often seem or even be limited without my questions ceasing to be intelligent and interesting, if they are good ecclesiological questions. Furthermore, years of reflections have taught me well that everything is connected! And everything is connected in the process of questioning as well as in our attempts at an answer.

The third constraint comes from the fact that, in trying to describe a general mentality, I have to function within a logic to which I am no longer accustomed. The analysis of our religious mentality constantly made me return to a schema which, proceeding from *God* to the *world* and passing through *Jesus Christ*, the *priests*, the *mass*, and the *church*, sets off a movement within which I feel cramped. One will doubtless understand this better when reading the book. I shall add, however, that this process had the advantage of furnishing the reflection with clear landmarks, with each theme providing the object of a distinct chapter. In any case, do we ever have the right to deny what is the real state of the church, of ecclesiology, and of present ecclesiastical structures, for example, in favor of what should be or, more precisely, in favor of what life already proposes, though without the clarity of the self-evident?

At first glance, the fourth constraint seems only to be a matter of terminology. I hope that the book will show that there is

A CHURCH OF THE BAPTIZED

more at issue than a matter of words. It is, in fact, difficult for me and theologically impossible to speak of *clerics* and *lay people*. These two terms refer to a type of relation which, of itself, makes clerics and lay people to exist *as* clerics and lay people. How could I still be at ease with each of these two terms when I challenge this relation? To put it crudely, I think that the future of the clergy and of the laity requires that the clerics cease being clerics and that lay people cease being lay people. Since this book analyzes from cover to cover a structure in which there are still clerics and lay people, I was obliged to maintain this terminology to the end. An even more difficult matter is that I never wanted to leave a real church, which is what it is, even if I ardently wish it to become something else.

One will perhaps guess that this fidelity, which is beyond words and quite the contrary of conformity, constitutes for me an essential condition for a true conversion of the church. Am I a good servant of this conversion? There arrives a moment when the only valid word is that of silence. But one certainly must not be silent too soon. Everyone should speak out again and again, even cry out if necessary, so that abandonment to the ineffable may not be an abdication before the challenge of history. I only hope that my book will serve this speaking and, in the long run, in the very long run, serve a silence filled with life. The weight of the march, the labor of reflection and writing, and, above all, the heaviness of consent to true life would then have meaning.

1

The Dimensions of the Question

In ecclesiastical life and organization today, a mass of concrete difficulties are referable to the binomial *clergy/laity*. From the wider to the more restricted, all the fields in which the church is active are affected. The universal church is being shaken by it. To take only one example, just think of the appeals launched by more and more women who no longer accept being "condemned to the laity" by the sole fact of their sexual identity. Within narrower limits, the problem is acutely posed for the dioceses and the parishes. Some are trying to make more space for lay people. But that often takes place at the price of tensions which, in the best of cases, make ecclesiastical life no longer have the calm self-evidence it had before and, in the worst, turn into conflicts which, one fears, may be fatal for the life of the diocesan or parish church. Do more restricted communities, which have arisen in a remarkable manner in the last few years (in Latin America, for example), escape these frictions? On the contrary, they inevitably become a sort of laboratory where clergy and laity are forced to rethink their relations and to open up, without a predefined itinerary, new ways of common ecclesiastical life.

In short, the pair "clergy/laity" poses a problem.[1] One cannot even count anymore the books and articles dedicated to the tremors that shake this ménage. For the moment, however, it should suffice to refer each one to his or her own experience. Who would be incapable today of finding facts that illustrate the malaise in question here? We are at a point where no one can escape the questions being posed, regardless of the answer being given in our conscious or unconscious minds.[2]

A CHURCH OF THE BAPTIZED

But have we really measured the challenge to be taken up? We always have the answers our questions deserve. More correctly, in order to enter upon the construction of ways that truly open up the future, one must first enter into the often disquieting world of questioning. With respect to clergy/laity relations, I do not believe that contemporary demands are always well understood. For my part, I should distinguish *three levels* of the problem, the third being the only one that clears the space necessary for a satisfactory unfolding of the question. On the first level, the difficulties experienced between clerics and lay people are seen as difficulties *of functioning*. One greatly enlarges the problem as soon as, on the second level, one begins to suspect that the *structure* itself of clergy/laity relationships must perhaps be challenged. Then, following this line, one penetrates into the third level, by far the most disquieting: Can one think of the clergy and the laity differently, organize their relationships in a new way, without challenging *the structure of the whole religious universe* of which we are the heirs? Personally, I believe that our fidelity to Jesus Christ and to the church demands that the process of questioning be carried that far. But that is not self-evident, and we must now retrace the course more attentively whose three great moments I have just marked out.

The First Level: Difficulties of Functioning

A first way of considering the difficulties that are experienced in clergy/laity relations is to see them exclusively as problems of *functioning*. One lives in a certain type of ecclesiastical organization, with a certain distribution of power and responsibilities between clerics and lay people, and this organization is not functioning very well. This being the case, the stakes are clear: it is necessary to *improve* the functioning of the organization.

THE DIMENSIONS OF THE QUESTION

Toward an Improvement of Clergy/Laity Relations

Either I am very mistaken, or this is the way the question is very generally posed. Let us take it up again on the level of parish life. For the vast majority of Christians today, in effect, the church still takes on the countenance of their parish and does so almost exclusively. And it is there first of all that the difficulties to which I have alluded are experienced concretely. It is there that the relations between clergy and laity seem strained, if they are not simply cut off. There is no need at all to refer to ecclesiastical folklore here, to those open fights everyone has heard of and which formerly pitted one person against another, a given parish priest against a given parishioner or parishioners. In one sense, these tensions have become commonplace today. But they do not tear the fabric of ecclesiastical life apart any less. It is clear, for example, that they have contributed to this sort of silent hemorrhaging that has emptied the parish churches. The dissatisfactions continue to mount nonetheless. Lay people complain about a boring liturgy where the priest does everything, about meaningless homilies, and, more generally, about a parish life over which the parish priest has complete control. For their part, several parish priests and vicars reproach lay people, whom they are unable to make budge, for their passivity, for a sort of ecclesiastical lethargy that prevents them from dedicating to the service of parish organizations energies that are generously activated elsewhere, etc. Something is evidently not *functioning* very well. Both priests and parishioners are constrained to conclude that it is necessary to *improve* the *functioning* of parish life (and the challenge presents a certain urgency everywhere). Here a committee will be set up that will advise parish priests and vicars in establishing pastoral priorities. There baptism and confirmation preparation will be entrusted to lay people in order to free ever more burdened priests or to create a better effective sharing of responsibilities. At mass one will have lay people come up into the

9

A CHURCH OF THE BAPTIZED

sanctuary for the proclamation of the word and other different services. In the boldest parishes, priests will even go so far as to entrust the homily to a non-priest in the hope that the word will cease being insignificant and will be better wed to those innumerable little words that conjugate human life in the present. In short, immense energies are being expended in order to improve parish life and the relationships between the clergy and the faithful.

Let us say that, in a general way, the same diagnosis is made on other levels of ecclesiastical organization and that the remedies suggested are of the same nature. A few quite fleeting encounters with their bishop do not suffice for the members of the diocese to put a face with his name, if they even know his name at all! One will thus be dedicated to favoring more frequent contacts and a better reciprocal acquaintance. A few diocesan newspapers, for example, will then give the agenda of the major pastoral activities of the bishop. Is it believed that Rome misunderstands the petitions arising from the diocesan and national churches? Certain episcopal conferences have complained of it, politely but with a certain courage. It is then demanded that the movement between these two poles be improved, particularly by taking maximum advantage of the incredible means of communication that modern technology places at our disposal.

These rapidly evoked illustrations and their analysis are lacking in refinement. Nevertheless, they should suffice for each one to return to his or her own experience and to name situations on his or her own in which problems of ecclesiastical life are reflected according to the logic that I have just described. What must be remembered here appears simple enough in the end. In the face of the difficulties that are experienced in the relationships between clerics and lay people, the following *diagnosis* is made: it is the *functioning* of these relationships that is causing the problem. The *stakes* are then clear and are defined in terms of *improvement*. But let us add a point of capital importance for what follows. One wishes to improve the way in which power and responsibilities are distributed today between clerics and lay people, *but while still respecting the way in which these relations are presently structured.* Logically, in effect, the language of improvement supposes that what should be improved is not challenged. One contents oneself with correcting the malfunctions and perfecting the organization. With respect to clergy/laity relations, one purifies them but *as they are presently structured.* Do they distribute power and responsibilities in the church in a certain way? This distribution should be improved—and thus fundamentally respected! Thus, one does not challenge the present structure of relationships.

Two Characteristics of This Approach

This way of seeing things has multiple implications. I shall content myself with underlining *two characteristics* that it inevitably gives to every process that tries to change something in the present state of clergy/laity relations.

It *"spiritualizes"* what is at stake and readily becomes *moralizing* in the end. Rather than confronting problems of a structural nature at their level, one jumps into a totally different area of the problem. One lets it be understood in a thousand ways, for example, or one clearly affirms that everything would be better in the church if the priests were holier, if the bishops and the pope were more open, if the clergy prayed more and divested itself of scandalous riches. To sum it up, ecclesiastical life will improve the day each cleric adopts attitudes and patterns of behavior that will reveal a little better this "other Christ" that he became by his ordination. One spiritualizes and moralizes just as much with respect to the laity. Lay people lack generosity; that is what explains their inertia and the feebleness of their commitment to the church. Would they dare, on the other hand, to affirm that their taking charge of parish life is a right and a responsibility? They are letting themselves be perverted by democratic ideals borrowed from the latest fashionable trends which cannot be

A CHURCH OF THE BAPTIZED

consonant with the hierarchical nature of the church. Even worse, the moral laxity of our civilization, especially in the realm of sexuality, has taken them hostage, and that is why they rise up against the official morality in realms such as birth control, premarital relations, homosexuality, etc.

The second implication is even more harmful. If the only challenge is to improve the present relationships between clerics and lay people, experience shows how one inevitably compartmentalizes ecclesiastical life by *individualizing* questions. As long as the structure is not challenged, the "true" questions will bear on *one or the other* of the two poles and not on the complex network where the fate of their mutual relationships is decided.

"Divide and rule better" seems to presuppose the dynamics of improvement. I know that the question raised here is a considerable one. It is, however, decisive for the future of the church, and no one has the right to silence it or to have it silenced. It concerns theological reflection as well as ecclesiastical life in its most everyday aspects. Speaking first of the clergy, I shall risk two illustrations, each one drawn from one of these two fields (life and reflection). Priests and bishops have made considerable efforts, especially since Vatican II, to define with greater precision their identifying traits: sessions on pastoral ministry, programs of theological reorientation, gatherings of priests which sometimes involve living together, setting up priests' councils and different episcopal commissions, synodal meetings, etc. The list of initiatives that have been taken is long and the energies have been expended without measure. But, nevertheless, the "crisis of priestly identity" seems to persist. Could this not be because all these initiatives have gathered priests and bishops *among themselves?* Will they rediscover the specific sense of their service as long as they do not *live* in the midst of a true community where they are first of all believers *with* other believing persons?

On the second level, that of reflection, I pose the same question. And I formulate the same reservations with respect to

12

the enormous literature that has been dedicated during the last thirty years to the "priesthood" of the priests and bishops. Theology has doomed itself to failure each time it has considered the priesthood as a thing-in-itself in a self-centered and individualizing fashion. And the only undertakings that promise a certain liberation are those (very rare ones) that try to reflect the service of priests and bishops *in their ties* to the baptismal priesthood.

One could say the same of the other pole and wonder to what the efforts to reevaluate the laity can lead as long as one does not redefine it (theoretically but also in the practice of ecclesiastical life) *in the relations* that it maintains with the clergy.[3]

However, the individualization of questions is even more manifest when it is a question of short-term relations. Does a difficulty arise in a certain parish? One will almost always attribute it to the malfunctioning of a *given* priest or to the stubbornness of a *given* parishioner; it is essentially due to a given individual or to a given group of individuals. But what if it were the present organization of parishes that structured the relations between laity and priests in such a way that these relations will always be a problem? Or, conversely, what if it were the present *relationships* between clergy and laity that fashioned a type of parish in which the ones and the others are a priori condemned to tensions and to sterile confrontations? This type of questioning is evidently unacceptable for those whose concerns are limited to improving the functioning of what already exists.

The Second Level: A Question of Ecclesiastical *Structures*

It is necessary to leave the language of improvement and, above all, the logic in which it stifles our ecclesiological problems. Life has furnished sufficient proof that in this respect the future (of both clerics and lay people) is blocked. Of course, there will always be room for improvement, and no one will ever be holy enough. But how can one not notice, on the one hand, that

A CHURCH OF THE BAPTIZED

many lay people begin to experience difficulties of relation to the clergy *at the very moment* they become more "generous," the day they decide to dedicate their time and energy to parish or diocesan life, or when they respond to the invitation issued to them to exercise concern for the whole church? On the other hand, one would have to be myopic, to make a rather short reading of the history of the church, in order to refuse to recognize that the present clergy is quite exemplary compared to the clergy of certain past centuries.

The question must be shifted. But in what direction? Are we totally lacking in our search for a possible orientation? A way was opened, at least implicitly, when I refused to *individualize* the questions. It does not, in effect, suffice to work on one pole *or* the other, to rethink the clergy *or* the laity, as if each one constituted an autonomous reality, a thing-in-itself from which the ecclesiastical future will be set in motion independently of the other pole. Difficulties arise *at the very heart of the relations* in play between clerics and lay people, and it is there that attention must be focused, there that correctives must be applied if necessary. More particularly, it is the *present structure* of these relations that requires attention, and nothing will change in ecclesiastical life as long as one refuses to bring the questions to bear on this precise spot.[4]

To put it clearly, a *structural defect* is putting a strain on clergy/laity relationships. This strain represents a defect which, independently of reciprocal good or bad will, pre-defines an ecclesiastical and ecclesiological place for each term and pre-determines a certain type of attitudes and patterns of behavior that one has a right to expect from clerics or lay people. In speaking of a structural defect, one is thus not evoking some theoretical problem of which only minds lost in the universe of a paralyzing abstraction are fond. It is a question here of a certain concrete organization of the church, one ideologically justified by a certain theology of the church, which commands

14

THE DIMENSIONS OF THE QUESTION

a certain type of relations between clerics and lay people—relations vitiated *in advance,* from which the one or the other will inevitably come out hurt, despite the best of good wills. Thus, it is evidently necessary to try to name this defect. Three moments will progressively clarify the question seeking to be expressed here.

A Significant Text

Why do so many priests and bishops feel *personally* attacked as soon as the present organization of the church is called into question? And why do so many lay people find the least critique of the clergy, and especially of the pope, insulting to the church? Doubtless because all have grown up in a church where these questions were not even formulable. Nothing suggests this so well as the text I am going to cite now which, even if it dates from the beginning of the century, speaks of the present, of the present state of the church, and of the idea that is still had of the church. It would be necessary to invent a new conjugation which would be the "past present." Once relieved of certain expressions that spontaneously repel one, a text of Pius X clearly introduces us into the universe to be explored, which, as we shall see later, continues to be our universe. Pius X writes:

> *It follows that the church is by essence an unequal* society, that is, a society comprising two categories of persons, the pastors and the flock, those who occupy a rank in the different degrees of the hierarchy and the multitude of the faithful. So distinct are these categories that with the pastoral body only rests the necessary right and authority for promoting the end of the society and directing all its members toward that end; the one duty of the multitude is to allow themselves to be led, and, like a docile flock, to follow the pastors (*Vehementer nos*).

A CHURCH OF THE BAPTIZED

The mere reading of this text sounds foreign to ears that have heard a different kind of talk at Vatican II; it causes an uneasy feeling. But an uneasy feeling is not a question. It is thus worthwhile to explain in detail the ecclesiological vision of Pius X, if only in order to help this uneasy feeling become a question. Five points in particular promise to give content to the structural defect that I am trying to define.

1. The church is "an *unequal* society," and that is the first point to remember. In the society of the church, there are (if one wishes to respect the logic of the inequality schema) a more and a less, a top and a bottom, with these binomials situating ecclesiastically "two categories of persons." The relations between clerics and lay people will thus have to respect the laws and implications of this inequality. This is to say that, even *before* relations between clergy and laity are formed (and, I am anxious to repeat, independently of reciprocal good or bad will), one is entitled to *expect* that these will be relations between a *more* which is *at the top* with respect to a *less* which is *at the bottom* and vice versa.

2. "The pastors," the members "of the hierarchy," "the pastoral body," are situated *at the top*. If the pope, the bishops, and the priests occupy such a place in ecclesiastical life and organization, it is because "the necessary right and authority for promoting the end of the society and directing all its members toward that end" are exhausted in them. Responsibility for the church and fidelity to the end it pursues are thus entrusted to them.

3. "The hierarchy" is itself hierarchized: it comprises "different degrees." At the risk of demonstrating it throughout the whole reflection, one is moving here within an extremely logical and coherent system. It can thus be presumed that the pope, the bishops, and the priests, who occupy different "degrees" in the hierarchy, will also maintain relationships of "inequality," relationships of a top and a bottom.

16

THE DIMENSIONS OF THE QUESTION

4. "The flock," "the multitude of the faithful," is the ecclesiastical bottom. What right does it have? It has no other than that of allowing itself "to be led." Its ecclesiastical responsibility and fidelity to the church are thus reduced to the duty imposed upon it of "following the pastors." Its only right is thus a right to passivity.

5. Finally, these relationships of inequality are commanded by the very *"essence"* of the church, and this point deserves to be strongly emphasized. Inequality is not a question of historical organization, valuable for a time but susceptible of correction and, ultimately, of disappearance. According to Pius X, inequality derives from the *nature* of the church; it constitutes an essential element of its definition. According to this logic, and despite the fact that one may be shocked by it, one is thus entitled to affirm that, as soon as the relationships of inequality between the pastors and the flock are denied and disappear, the church is no longer faithful to itself; it denies itself and disappears as the church.

An Exclusively Deductive Movement

This last remark suggests very well the amplitude of the question that one tackles when one attempts to rethink clergy/laity relations. A rapid and superficial view will judge that this question is second and secondary. With the depth of ideological justification that has been given to the present structure of relations between clerics and lay people, every question about this organization inevitably leads, in fact, to questioning the very heart of the church and its nature.[5]

Pius X is a witness of a long past; he reflects a general mentality that has been slowly forged in the course of centuries.[6] Taking notice of this historical density, one can advance two remarks that are of importance for life and reflection. On the one hand, this long past has so marked the church that, as I suggested above, everyone must surely conjugate it in the pres-

A CHURCH OF THE BAPTIZED

ent. We are the children of this tradition, both in what we reject and in what we accept. Who, under the pretext of delivering the church from a vision judged to be alienating, can claim to have been liberated himself or herself in such a rapid and definitive way from that which he or she refuses and condemns? On the other hand, one understands the reluctance, even the fear, that certain ones experience as soon as the present organization of clergy/laity relations is challenged. It is their vision of the church that is being threatened. And the tie that they have established between their life and the church, however loose it may be, introduces a doubt into the very meaning they wished to give to their existence.

Far from discouraging this process, this second remark should stimulate it. Fear is not conquered by arbitrarily forcing the questions that give rise to it into silence. Ultimately, then, these questions bear on the nature of the church. More immediately, however, they affect the *ecclesiastical identity* of clerics and lay people respectively. If this identity emerges from their relations, how are the latter organized, and what place do they make for each member of the binomial within the structure of common ecclesiastical life?

Identified by their right and authority, clerics have the power to "promote and direct"; they are invested with everything necessary for the society of the church to march toward its end. In their relationships with lay people, they can only stand *at the beginning* of the relation. Furthermore, lay people stand at the term and *can only stand at the term* of the movement since their *only* right is to let themselves be led and to follow the clerics. One thus has the following literary schema: clergy→laity, with the arrow indicating a unidirectional movement.

Since it is a question of "inequality," if we keep in mind the ranks that situate the different degrees of the hierarchy, the unicity of direction may take another spatial translation as well:

18

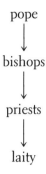

Of course, one will have recognized the ecclesiological schema and the mode of functioning of a *pyramidal* and *clerical church*. As soon as one ceases to let oneself be hypnotized by each of the terms and considers the movement indicated by the arrows instead, one sees that *this movement only goes and can only go from the top to the bottom*. It is in this sense that it is necessary to speak of an *exclusively deductive* movement. This is what the structural defect consists in that I am trying to name. At the top, the clergy monopolizes the having (they "possess" the "things" of the faith), the knowledge, and the power, whereas a priori lay people have nothing, know nothing, and can do nothing. Clerics have and are able to give; lay people have not and can only receive. Has, for example, the fact been sufficiently pondered that, concretely speaking, *all* the power is today still in the hands of the hierarchy, the legislative power, the executive power, and the judicial power? Will one be able to reevaluate the laity without treading on what seems to be considered the private ground of the clergy? But what form would the exercise of power then take in the church? Another illustration: For centuries, theological knowledge has been considered the proper possession of the clergy. And the phenomenon of lay people teaching in faculties of theology is very recent. In canonical faculties, they must still have a mandate from the bishop. In the Catholic

A CHURCH OF THE BAPTIZED

denomination, lay people have even been refused a direct access to scripture by prohibiting, for example, that the Bible be translated into the so-called common languages.

One could pursue the string of illustrations indefinitely and write a catalogue of recriminations that a more and more numerous host of lay people are expressing. Furthermore, each one can probably draw up his or her own list of experienced frustrations. Let it suffice to repeat what was affirmed above and now takes on sharper contours: One cannot and one will not be able to rethink the laity, to give it an ecclesiastical place that is more just from a Christian viewpoint, without revising the structure of its relations to the clergy. For it is precisely *there* that what is truly at stake is decided, that which has some chance of concretely transforming the life of the church. If the present structure of relationships is not changed, every invitation that clerics issue to lay people will be understood as an attempt at the "clergification" of the laity. In fact, more and more lay people are becoming conscious of this threat, particularly when it is a question of a permanent diaconate and, more generally, of what are called "the new ministries." Another point becomes evident as a result: nothing is resolved, nothing will be resolved, if one only *inverts the terms without changing the movement.* Lay people could be put on the top and clerics on the bottom, but that would only produce a new form of the pyramidal church, a new clericalism: clerics would no longer be those who are designated as such, but other clerics would arise, other holders of power and knowledge, who would nourish the same type of ecclesiological logic and ecclesiastical structure.

A Subject and an Object of Ecclesiastical Life

What has just been said may seem to yield rather meager results in the end. Other analyses, doubtless more subtle, have already denounced this defect of a clerical church and of an exclusively deductive logic. But an additional step is now possible. What is the ecclesiastical defect of the structure that has been disengaged? It is the establishment of relations in which the clergy is the subject, whereas the lay people, who can only follow and receive, are reduced to the condition of an object. More precisely, it is making clerics the only true *subject* of the church and condemning lay people to the condition of an *object*.

As the only active guarantor of its relations with lay people, clerics constitute the sole active and responsible subject (one will excuse the tautology: there is no subject who is not active and responsible) of the historical existence of the church. That is another statement that may seem banal, but its impact will be absolutely immense, if one measures all its implications. It is thus worthwhile to render explicit, at least rapidly, three characteristics that define clerics in their condition as subject of the church.

1. As a subject, the pope, the bishops, and the priests are *authorized to conjugate the verbal phrase "to-be-church" in the first person of the present indicative.* They can say: "*We are* the church." Life has so anchored this view of things in individual and collective mentalities that language continues to *identify* church and clergy. A given television broadcast, for example, will focus on the sexual morality of the church without asking even once either among the experts or the general viewing public *who* is the defining subject of this morality said to be "of the church," when more than half the Christians concerned claim to be in disagreement with this morality. Furthermore, even today one can always presume that if a newspaper article is headed by a title referring to the church, it will focus concretely on the acts and deeds of a (collective or individual) member of the clergy: "The church takes a stand on . . ."

2. As subjects of the church, the pope, the bishops, and the priests can equally affirm: "We are *responsible* for the church." One is not a true subject if one is not responsible for that of which one claims to be a subject. Thanks in particular to the concentra-

A CHURCH OF THE BAPTIZED

tion of power of which I have spoken, the clergy remain in fact *the ones* responsible for ecclesiastical life. If necessary, they will be able to "commission" lay people, invite them to "share in" their responsibility, but in doing so, as the terminology already betrays, they only confirm the exclusivity of their own responsibility.

3. The third point is so important that all that follows will be the explicitation of it: clerics are the *historical* subject of the church. They may refer to a-temporal principles, claim a-historical justifications, sometimes evoke the "will of God" to justify any one of their modes of being and operating. But they remain creatures of flesh and blood who are historically defined, and it is of the church of history that they are concretely the historical subject.

As for lay people, they are nothing ecclesiastically. The deductive logic and the structure it justifies condemn them to the status of a *passive object* (another tautology). Clerics have everything, and lay people have value only through that which is given to them and which they receive (their "only right," said Pius X, is to let themselves be led and to follow their pastors). Let us say it clearly: The ecclesiastical identity of lay people comes from their capacity to seek "elsewhere" (in the clergy) the meaning of their membership in the church.

From this point of view, to take only one illustration, catechisms have formed such deep convictions that it would be magic if the ecclesiastical mentality were totally liberated from them today. I shall cite the *Catéchisme de Poitiers* for a single reason: it has the advantage of saying in a short formula what the other catechisms take much time to unfold. Furthermore, it would be necessary to take up again here that which introduced the text of Pius X above: it is of a *"past present"* that I am speaking in citing this catechism, as I shall have occasion to show immediately. The *Catéchisme de Poitiers* asks: "How do you know that you are members of the true church?" The question bears on the ecclesiastical *identity* of lay people, on the certainty they do or do not

22

have of belonging to the "true church." They have been taught to respond: "I know that I am a member of the true church *because* I am united to my parish priest, and my parish priest is united to the bishop, who is himself united to the pope."[7] The "because" is clear: it is insofar as one refers to someone else (the parish priest, then the bishop, then the pope) that one can know one is a member of the true church. And that is where, in my opinion, this catechism speaks of the present mentality. How many Christians of our day spontaneously anchor the church in their act of faith itself, an act that is always personal (let us add: and thus always communal) and can never be passively abandoned into the hands of someone else, whoever he may be?

Since I often cite this text of the *Catéchisme de Poitiers*, I know from experience the surprise and even the mockeries that it provokes today. In a very short time, thanks in particular to Vatican II, the ecclesiastical consciousness has undergone such transformations that the response of the catechism seems to take some back to that distant obscurantism which they themselves have left behind. But the mockery is out of place; the question is serious and poses, in short, a challenge that we at the end of the twentieth century are far from having accepted. In effect, for a long time lay people have become accustomed to an experience of *disappropriation*. They have learned to know themselves ecclesiastically *by that which they are not* (i.e. the clerics). Should we be surprised that it is still difficult for them today to exercise their responsibility in the existence and the life of the church? Are certain priests or bishops shocked by the reluctance of lay people to welcome a church that one now wishes to put back into its hands? But it is relatively easy to say to them today: "You are the church!" This proposition, however, meets with a disappropriation that is several centuries old. How much time will it take to pass from the condition of an *object* to that of a *subject*?

A final point, but not the least, is that in the logic we have evoked the definition of the laity *does not and cannot have a*

A CHURCH OF THE BAPTIZED

positive content. Defined by others, in its relation to that which (or those who) *it is not,* the laity seeks in vain a specific nature that will positively express its ecclesiastical identity. This has been reported several times: the notion of the laity "was purely negative; the sole distinctive criterion of the lay person was that of not being clergy and that of being defined by a lack, not by his or her own ministry."[8] Beyond the report, however, one can advance as a principle the fact that lay people's search for identity is really hopeless (because condemned to failure in advance) if the defect I have just named is not corrected, if the present organization of their relations to the clergy is not transformed.

The last council wished to attempt a positive definition of the laity—in section 31 of *Lumen Gentium,* for example. In fact, the first paragraph of this section advances several "statements" whose sole weakness is that it is difficult to see how they do not equally concern clerics. By the lay people one should in effect understand Christians who "are by baptism made one body with Christ and are established among the people of God. They are in their own way made sharers in the priestly, prophetic, and kingly functions of Christ. They carry out their own part in the mission of the whole Christian people with respect to the church and the world." This passage simply affirms a way that would be proper to lay people ("in their own way"). But that does not constitute an answer, since this is precisely the question that must be posed: What is proper to the laity? Who can say what its way is and define its ecclesiastical status? Through its lack of content, then, this sentence does not succeed in correcting the negative character of this other sentence that immediately precedes it and that illustrates what has just been said about the negative character that burdens the definition of the laity: "The term laity is here understood to mean all the faithful except those in holy orders and those in a religious state sanctioned by the church."

A second paragraph follows that insists on the "secular quality" of lay people in order to render explicit their "proper and

THE DIMENSIONS OF THE QUESTION

special" character. But what is there in this paragraph that would not apply to clerics as well? Everything turns around the statement according to which "the laity, by their very vocation, seek the kingdom of God by engaging in temporal affairs and by ordering them according to the plan of God." For their part, "those in holy orders" remain "chiefly and professedly ordained to the sacred ministry." But unless we deny that the Christian faith affirms the historicity of the sacred in general and of the church in particular, the sacred and the church constitute *temporal* realities, and the clergy is thus also devoted to "engaging in temporal affairs." How could "temporality" truly answer the question raised by the first paragraph on the ecclesiastical identity of the laity?

It is an undeniable fact that Vatican II has introduced considerable changes in ecclesiastical life and reflection on the church and, as such, has opened spaces the exploration of which is far from being finished. We, however, remain responsible to this council, and, as one may guess, this responsibility is not reduced to the function of being mimics or megaphones. We are perhaps responsible for our fidelity to the *dynamics* that the council set under way rather than bound to a conformity to the letter of the texts, if only to clarify a point so essential as that of the ecclesiastical identity of the laity.[9]

The Third Level: A *Religious Universe* To Be Rethought

Ecclesiastical relations are thus organized in such a way that both clerics and lay people, a priori and even before actually entering into relation, expect clerics to be the subject of these relations.[10] They expect the pope, the bishops, and the priests to hold true ecclesiastical responsibility, that which is finally decisive for the life of the church. This structuring has commanded and still commands the concrete organization of the ecclesiastical institution at all levels of this organization. Furthermore, the

A CHURCH OF THE BAPTIZED

passivity of lay people has also been inscribed, as it were, within the organization and to such an extent that one notices more and more an at least paradoxical phenomenon: as soon as some (lay people or members of the clergy) wish to introduce changes in the present organization of relationships, it is often lay people who rise up to demand that "the right order" be reestablished and thus that their right to passivity be respected.

Once again, the second level does not pose a judgment of the moral order; it does not wish to decide between good and bad wills. It only notices that an organization is there in its density as an historical datum and lets it be understood that a call to convert minds and hearts doubtless does not suffice for the concrete functioning of the church to change. These calls to conversion are futile as long as they are not accompanied by an effective transformation of the ecclesiastical structures.

To state clearly what I think and believe I have shown: there would be no "lay people" in the church if there were no "clerics." I should specify, however, that clerics and lay people only exist *as* clerics and *as* lay people in virtue of a structure of relations that constitutes them as such. In my opinion, ecclesiological reflection makes this evident, but the relationships that are lived daily in the concrete functioning of ecclesiastical life, in the parishes, in the dioceses, and wherever clerics and lay people enter into relation perhaps do so even more. All that follows must evidently bear the burden of proof; it will validate or invalidate this judgment.[11]

When one agrees to enter into questions of structure, the field is considerably enlarged, and one comes to the third level of the problem. I know of no theologian who has ventured there in even a slightly systematic manner. But the amplitude of the question of the laity then appears in the simple formulation of the following hypothesis: *the present structure of clergy/laity relations also organizes the whole complex network of the relations that constitute our religious mentality.* As I said before, the laity

THE DIMENSIONS OF THE QUESTION

cannot be thought of in itself, nor can the clergy either; it is their *relations* that are the problem. What is now new, the step that the hypothesis invites one to take, could be formulated for the moment in the following way: even the clergy/laity relations will not change if one is content to consider them in themselves, independently of the relations that weave the whole of our religious universe, from our relations to God to our relations to the world.

The Structure of our Religious Mentality

In order for this hypothesis to begin to speak, one will have to evoke (even if, for the moment, this evocation is still rough) the religious structure of which we are the heirs and which has marked and still marks in a general way the so-called Christian mentalities. The very serious *Dictionnaire de théologie catholique* is a good witness of our heritage. What does one have to do, the *Dictionnaire* asks, when one wishes "to demonstrate the truth of the Catholic Church"? One must essentially "demonstrate that the Christian revelation has been entrusted by Jesus Christ to an authority to which he himself has assigned clearly defined properties and that this divinely established authority exists solely in the Catholic Church, the only true Church of Jesus Christ."[12] The revelation of God has thus been entrusted by Jesus Christ to the clergy, and it is the latter that has the authority to define the truth of the church of history. Schematically, the realities begin to be organized in this way: God→Jesus Christ→hierarchy→church.

Historically, one must add, the authority of the clergy has been given a particular theoretical and practical basis as power over the mass (I shall speak of this again in the following chapter). By introducing this new pole, one completes the religious landscape in which the vast majority of Christians today have grown up. And one can disengage these principal articulations: *God*, through *Jesus Christ*, gives to the *clergy* a power over the *mass*. It is in the mass that the *church* truly realizes the fullness of its

27

A CHURCH OF THE BAPTIZED

mystery. And it is from there that, nourished by the mass, it can go to the *world*.

What is more important than the fact of naming the elements of the landscape is grasping the logic and the movement that organize their relations. We have no choice but to recognize, through the simple description that has just been made, that we find the same structuring as found in clergy/laity relations themselves: the entire landscape obeys an *exclusively deductive movement*. This observation thus permits us to complete the schema begun above:

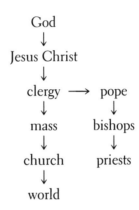

We thus find that the structure that pre-determined clergy/laity relations now organizes the whole of our religious universe. The hypothesis is thus taking shape in the sense that one can already presume that *each element will be considered as a passive object in its relations with the top and as an active subject of its relations with the bottom.*

For the Continuation of the Reflection

One can expend enormous amounts of energy in reflecting on each of the elements of the schema. The element of the hierarchy, in particular, has attracted a considerable amount of

THE DIMENSIONS OF THE QUESTION

attention in the last few decades, as the bibliography of theological writings testifies. But our heritage situated each element within an extremely coherent universe (which the schema sufficiently suggests). It was understood according to a logic that articulated the whole of the Christian religious mentality. Consequently, the question evidently becomes how to have an effect on one element, and what chance there is of truly rethinking it and restoring it ecclesiastically (of redefining, for example, its place in the hierarchy of the church), if the *logic* is not questioned and if the other poles continue to be articulated among themselves as they were before.

Hence this other question which bears this time on the particular subject of the laity: Can one expect to understand better the ecclesiastical and ecclesiological status of lay people without an at least minimal reflection on the other poles and, above all, on the way in which their relations are articulated? For that is what the ideological apparatus consists, in that it serves to justify clericalism. Beyond a particular pole and the lot that it reserves for lay people, the articulation of the elements and the overall coherence are woven in such a tight way that one cannot see anything else of the laity than what it *is not*. A significant index of this is that the laity is not found among the elements of the schema that I have just sketched. Did I voluntarily omit speaking of it? In its way, this absence means rather the concrete absence of lay people in the movement that structures the organization and the life of the church. And that means, conversely, that clarity will not be gained on the ecclesiastical situation of the laity without again placing the global religious logic in question. It would be wise to become as clearly conscious of this as possible, if only to avoid exhausting oneself in the pursuit of objectives that are unattainable a priori.

The continuation of the present reflection wishes particularly to question the overall logic and the structure of religious relationships. It will evidently not shed a satisfying light either on

29

A CHURCH OF THE BAPTIZED

each of the poles or on the ties that place them in relation. For that, an entire reflection on God, a christology, an anthropology, an ecclesiology, etc. would be necessary (which should be clear by now). My intention is more modest. I wish to indicate a task rather than to carry it to completion: to see how the question of the laity is situated today within an encompassing logic and to suggest paths (nothing more) that will open up the future of the laity and will give a future to the efforts that some, lay people especially, are making today in order to situate themselves better in the church.

I admit that a double suspicion is carrying my reflection. On the one hand, are not clergy/laity relations the *mirror image* of the structure that organizes the totality of our religious mental universe? On the other hand, it seems that precisely these relations *reinforce and nourish* the logic of the whole and, more concretely, our way of managing our historical relationships with God, Christ, the church, etc. That is perhaps why one hesitates so much to rethink the place assigned to lay people in the church. One guesses, even if confusedly, that the religious mental structures will not come away intact from this enterprise of truth.

With respect to the course adopted, it will be simple and unsatisfying in itself, but sufficient for the limited objective pursued here to be attained.[13] The following chapters will take up again the elements of the schema (God, Christ, etc.), successively and according to the order the logic has determined. And each chapter will pose three questions. The first one is: How is this pole generally understood *in its relations* to the others? I shall speak here of our immediate heritage, the one that has shaped our religious mentality and continues to mark Christian persons and communities, especially those of the Catholic confession. The second question is: How do *clergy/laity relations* reflect and nourish today the relations of each element to the whole? And finally: *What challenges* does the question of the laity propose today when it is situated in its ties with this or that element of our

30

THE DIMENSIONS OF THE QUESTION

religious mentality? Lived faith and theological reflection are in effect beginning to announce something different about God, Christ, and the other elements. Life and reflection, often in poverty, are opening other perspectives than those to which one was accustomed, and it is at least necessary to indicate the ecclesiastical future that they promise to those who continue to be called "lay people."

2

God

"To the Clergy the Sacred, to the Laity the Profane"

At the beginning, there is God. For my part, I think that a great majority of Christians continue to have a properly *theistic* conception of God. They situate him at the top of the schema, at the beginning, as the first element of the chain, the person on whom all the other elements depend and from whom there proceeds the place that each one occupies respectively in the schema. God is the absolute beginning. If the expression were not so inelegant, one could say more correctly that God is very generally seen as *an absolute of beginning.* Nothing and no one, being situated below in the chain of elements, will attain the status of subject or will be able to begin acting in history if God himself does not intervene each time to confer this privilege. "Theism," Raymond Winkling writes, "supposes the representation of a God in the beyond who is conceived of as a personal God. This personal God is supposed to have created the world and to be directing its evolution *by intervening from without* in the unfolding of events and the lives of individuals."[1] This citation brings out the extent to which God is a party to the exclusively *deductive* movement that we have discussed. God is its first and last justification. He constitutes the absolute condition of possibility of a logic where everything goes from the top toward the bottom.

Is not setting out from there going back too far in order to pose the particular question of the laity? On the contrary, far from being foreign to clergy/laity relations, the vision of God constitutes its ultimate and decisive pre-determination. In the common mentality, as we shall see further on, God intervenes directly to elevate clerics to the condition of subject of the church. That tells us to what extent the following question deserves to be posed: Is the passivity of lay people not justified in the last analysis by the conception we have of God?

1.   A Liberating God or an Alienating God?

Who is God as he exists in himself? Only a leap beyond humanity, beyond the historical limits that follow human beings like their shadows, would permit one to enter the universe of God and to speak from God's own point of view. Yet perhaps faith permits us to take this leap? That would only be possible in virtue of a schizophrenic dichotomization. It would, in effect, be presupposed that there is faith on one side, a place of clarity, which permits a direct access to God. This faith would then make do in other respects as well as it could with a limited humanity condemned to the determinations and abandoned to the hazards of a history that finds itself denied such a direct access to God.

A perfectly legitimate question, however, one with which one must absolutely concern oneself, is that of the *image* of God. What image of God do Christians have toward the end of the twentieth century, and what *relations to God* does this image create?

At the Beginning Is God

Let us first listen to the language that people spontaneously employ when they say "God." Most of the time they speak of God as an *absolute, goodness itself* or *the good Lord,* the *all-powerful.* Those more and more numerous people whom all forms of esotericism attract (and who often continue to call themselves Christians) utilize a vocabulary that posits God as the *supreme being,* if that much. In the movement Alcoholics Anonymous,

A CHURCH OF THE BAPTIZED

which originated and flourished in so-called "Christian" societies, the space is organized more explicitly by speaking of God familiarly as *"the guy upstairs."*

All these expressions, and many others, reveal that God is considered above all as the *transcendent*. He is the one up above who is all, does all, and is capable of all. He is *the* subject par excellence, alone capable of giving meaning to a (personal or collective) human history which, without him, is delivered up to incoherence. A logic is thus initiated according to which the world and history are all the more condemned to insignificance as the entire meaning of life is invited to be relocated in God. Everything can only proceed from God, and nothing beautiful or good can live that does not come directly from him.

I shall immediately indicate two characteristics that these images have impressed on the religious mentality and that command a type of relationship with the sacred with which we are still struggling today.

The images that are usually conveyed make God seem quite *distant*. In order to save God's transcendence, to safeguard it as an absolute beginning and an absolute of beginning, it is necessary to distance him from the universe of limits. God is truth itself, the all-beautiful, the all-good, and human existence is far from radiating absolute truth, beauty, and goodness. In one sense, the more a human being becomes conscious of one's own limits (which should be the fruit of maturation, even if maturity is evidently not reduced to this consciousness), the more he or she is led to hold God at bay from history. An entire anthropology has been articulated according to this dynamic, and from this point of view nothing is accidental or has the nature of insignificant detail. The construction of churches, for example, is revealing. These buildings have, in effect, laid out the space in such a way that they render the distance visible, the remoteness of "the presence": there is a long nave to be traversed, then a balustrade that separates, steps to be climbed, a long sanctuary, with steps at the very end, which lead to an altar, where the tabernacle is placed, the latter being itself veiled and hiding a presence that one cannot see or touch. Centuries have nourished such a relationship with the eucharist and the presence of God in the eucharist. Is one not justified in thinking that the anthropological schemas were simply upset the day it was permitted to receive communion in the hand? That is why it is so essential to grasp the logical links and the overall coherences. The same holds for our most concrete pastoral initiatives, and one cannot tamper with old mental machinery as one does with a physical object.

Strangeness still characterizes the God of spontaneous images. As absolute transcendence, God is that which believers see quite well that they are not. That too is said anthropologically and has commanded particular historical attitudes and behaviors. For centuries, for example, did not God speak Latin, a language that had become *foreign* and thus *strange* to the masses of the faithful? This strangeness is not so innocent as it appears: it served to distance God, to consolidate his transcendence by a retrenchment that, at the same time, instituted a break with the people and reinforced the absoluteness of his transcendence, by absolutizing, be it understood, the words of those who spoke the language! Who does not remember those times, which are not so ancient, when every sermon began with a Latin citation of which the people understood nothing, but which buttressed the words of the preacher on the foundation of an absolute authority: God himself was going to speak!

What shall we conclude from this? The general Christian mentality functioned (and still functions) within a logic of reified, physical causality and sees God as the *first cause* in the chain of causes. All the other links of the chain (Christ, clerics, eucharist, etc.) are *effects*, or, if they are elevated to the condition of *causes*, it is by a leap into the order of absolute transcendence, a displacement for which the first cause alone is immediately responsible. In a word, God is *the only truly active subject of everything*.

A CHURCH OF THE BAPTIZED

Condemned to Passivity

This vision of God reflects and commands a certain type of *relations to him*. And that is where the perversity of such a God begins to be experienced. The other chapters will situate the relationship of each one of the other elements of the schema with this absolute top. For the moment, because of the image of God as an *absolute of beginning,* it is possible to speak more globally of the "bottom," of history, of persons and collectivities who live there and work there. Four points in particular qualify the type of relations to God that Christians have been accustomed to live.

"Good" relations, those that are spontaneously experienced as pleasing to God, are, at bottom, those where God seems *to be self-evident.* Being considered absolute beauty and purity and the sole truth, God is encountered in all that one finds beautiful, good, and true in life. An entire anthropological vision has thus been constructed that continues to impose itself on consciences and to ravage lives. For example, it spatializes in the body a top (from the neck upward), which is the noble part and is worthy to form relations to God, and a bottom (from the neck downward), where what in fact are called the "private parts" are found. On the other hand, time is as organized as space. God is, as it were, localized in those privileged moments that seem filled with a sort of plenitude: amazement before a stunningly beautiful landscape, emotion felt on experiencing the attitudes and gestures of an exceptional goodness, rare but rich warm moments where the truth seems to be made, where one feels at peace with oneself. A profound truth of being is then experienced where the dream we all cherish of feeling our life to be like a beautiful round sphere without breaks, holes, or bumps is realized, even if only for too short an instant. God is indubitably there. It is self-evident, one would say. But, in that case, what becomes of God on those much more numerous days when nothing is self-evident? Has faith not slipped over into fideism? The proof of this would be the brevity of the answers given to two nevertheless fundamental

36

questions. So many people experience the days of doubt as a "disappearance of God" and thus as a "loss of faith." But does not the possibility of doubt constitute an essential dimension of the act of believing?[2] Furthermore, are the ties between faith and human *decision* really seen, that decision which rightly characterizes the status of the subjects of history? By closing God in where he seems self-evident, one ends up forgetting that to believe, especially in moments of doubt when nothing is self-evident anymore, is also *"to decide* to believe, to decide *to continue* to believe."[3]

It continues to be thought, then, that such are "good" relations to God, those where it is self-evident that God is encountered. Since everything is connected, one is led to a second type of considerations. They concern the fate that is then assigned to the bottom, to the *limits* of history. At the very least, Christians are spontaneously led to think that the limits are the very thing that do not interest God and that they thus cannot constitute a place of encounter with him. As pure transcendence, God is, as it were, the opposite of limits, the fullness of our voids. Even worse, these images betray the fact that God is often only the flip side of our human frustrations. Do not the limits end by being perceived as an *obstacle* that is interposed between God and humanity, that it is necessary to clear, or that one must rid oneself of in order to pass over to God's side? One illustration of this is the long-standing habits that have been inculcated in the life of prayer and in the place that is given there to the body. As a radical limit, the body is harmful to "mental" prayer. It is an obstacle that prevents one from entering into the universe of gratuitous relations to God. It especially should be forgotten, and a whole series of techniques have been elaborated to permit one to overcome its limits, to forsake it, to clear this obstacle in order finally to move within the true world, that of God.

The third point takes account of the *unhealthy guilt* that these images of God and the relations they favor have caused and

A CHURCH OF THE BAPTIZED

still cause. There is a healthy guilt, that which arises when love has been voluntarily killed or injured. Unhealthy, pathological guilt is that of the one who feels guilty for *being limited*. One cannot tell enough the ravages that are still caused by certain images of God in this area especially. And, no doubt, a long exercise in lucidity about oneself is necessary before someone can conclude that he or she has been liberated from them. Recently, in the space of a single day, there came to me three illustrations, at once eloquent and overwhelming. First there was an elderly man who had just lost his wife and, torn apart, sought why God had punished him so. Then there was a mother whose son had given himself up to drugs; she literally asked: "What have I done to the good Lord for this to happen to me?" Finally there was a youth who was quite disturbed because he experienced as a sin the sexual urges that he was incapable of silencing. These are the monstrosities to which our theistic visions of God lead. Raymond Winkling writes again: "Theism made the mistake of becoming an ideology that discharges man from his responsibilities in the face of human suffering: it presents God as the one on whom there depend good fortune and bad fortune, suffering and injustice, and, in this way, it furnished a comfortable alibi for refusing to commit oneself."[4] Catholics have had the reputation of nourishing these pathological inclinations: "You Catholics with your hell, your continually making people feel guilty, the exaggerated importance you give to sexual matters, you feel a judge's stare weighing upon you. You have instilled this fear in people."[5] Is this a thing of the past? An attentive look at the structure of our religious mentality should put us on guard against too rapid and definitive exorcisms. Catechesis, for example, wished to deliver us from this judge's stare that weighs upon our lives, and it began to speak of the God of love. But a certain understanding of love, or, more precisely, a certain place it is made to hold in the dynamics of human relations, can cause a guilt that is worse than the preceding ones. There are ways of speaking of the God of love which, in the concrete and because they do not convert the relation to God, absolutely condemn human loves, which are always fragile, poor, and small.

The fourth point prolongs the first three and concludes that there is no worse alienation than that caused by relations where God serves as a referent for absolutizing human passivity. These relations understand the absoluteness of God in such a way that *God becomes the very foundation of the status of passive object that is granted to human beings.* This is something that has undeniably been operative in the understanding of the Christian faith. Are Christians today still victims of this? One should at least open up enough space for the question to arise. Charles Bukowski, the American poet, deserves to be listened to here: "Nothing was ever in tune. People just blindly grabbed at whatever there was: communism, health foods, zen, surfing, ballet, hypnotism, group encounters, orgies, biking, herbs, Catholicism, weight-lifting, travel, withdrawal, vegetarianism, India, painting, writing, sculpting, composing, conducting, backpacking, yoga, copulating, gambling, drinking, Christ, TM, H, carrot juice, suicide, handmade suits, jet travel, New York City, and then it all evaporated and fell apart. People had to find things to do while waiting to die. I guess it was nice to have a choice."[6] These words lose their appearance of a theologically insignificant parenthesis as soon as one becomes aware that Bukowski is speaking here of western societies and thus of people who have grown up in the so-called "Christian" tradition. Why is there this precipitation that pushes people today to "grab blindly at whatever there is"? Let us note further that "Christ" and "Catholicism" figure as two of the elements among the several in the list of lifebelts. Is it not because allegedly Christian persons saw God first of all as a lifebelt who was to intervene directly all the time and in every moment of time? Since this belt saved nothing and "then it all fell apart," God disappears, and one divinizes something else in the hope that life will finally "be self-evident."

A CHURCH OF THE BAPTIZED

2. "To the Priests the Sacred, to the Laity the Profane"

It is on this structure of relations to God that one builds in order to give a radical justification to the respective place of clerics and of lay people in the church and, above all, the type of relationship that still presently structures their common ecclesiastical life. But one can also ask from the opposite side: Does not the present organization of the church even in its most concrete modes of functioning nourish an understanding of the absolute activity of God who absolutely sanctions the structural passivity of lay people?

Taken Up on the Side of God

The bishops and the priests have become "men *of God*," men *of the sacred*, and, under perhaps different forms, they still see themselves or are considered as such.

The French school of spirituality has played a considerable role in the formation of numerous generations of priests; many still practicing clerics have been formed according to this spirituality. I shall begin with a citation that furnishes a caricature which would lead one today to think of what the French school proposed. One of its champions, Mr. Tronson, exhorts priests in this way: "The cleric should be blind with respect to this world, not considering its beauties or its rarities at all. He should be deaf to its news, trample its pomps and vanities under foot, condemn all its tricks. We must regard ourselves as persons outside the world who live in heaven, who converse with the saints, who live in oblivion, in disdain, in contempt, and by an aversion to and sovereign condemnation of the entire age."[7]

The dichotomy is evident. Clerics have been taken up entirely on the side of God. For a long time they have learned to situate themselves *outside* the world and to live in heaven "conversing with the angels." With respect to the world below, clerics are invited to forget it, to disdain it, and even to hold it in

40

contempt. All that is said about it is that they should trample under foot its pomps and vanities and its tricks. Do clerics today resist these schizophrenic urges? Many among bishops and priests as well as among the lay people wish today that clerics would return to the realm of history. But they will not come back from such a long exile in just a few years.

Two characteristics burdened the images of God: *distance* and *strangeness*. They also left their mark on clerics, who have become men of God, and who are far from being delivered—if it is the case that they wish to exit from an alienating sacred realm at all, and provided that they be permitted to effect this return to the world and to history. Held at a distance from the masses of the faithful and accustomed to converse with the angels, they experience in their own flesh how difficult it is for them to be close to lay people now and to learn today the language of men. Certain persons and certain groups even want to forbid them this apprenticeship a priori, so much is one unaccustomed to see them take interest in the immediate challenges of humanity. Do the bishops, for example, dare say a word about the management of political and economic affairs? It is denied *from the beginning* that they can have any competence in these matters, and they are asked to return to their own affairs which are those of worship. And how many priests, at the heart of human relations, where they have gone incognito, so to speak, have seen these relations profoundly disturbed at the unveiling of their ecclesiastical status? One has not been accustomed to seeing them so close, concerned about the things of the world, and having some competence in the way they are conducted.

Being distanced, they appeared equally strange. Their being, their action, and their speech were marked with the strangeness of persons who, because they are "specialists of the sacred," do not work the way the rest of the world does, speak "the language of God" (Latin), do not dress like their brothers in humanity, and inhabit a strange place, the rectory.

A CHURCH OF THE BAPTIZED

Is the church now healed? Have clerics returned to human history? One can presume that this task will not be accomplished as long as priests and bishops are not willing to define themselves by the bottom, by a world arbitrarily situated below. The question at issue here is an entirely fundamental one. The ecclesiastical status of clerics and lay people will not be very well clarified as long as one does not begin to answer it. But this answer is itself dependent on the answer that is given to another question, one that is prior since it asks about the images of God: Is it true that nothing that is humanly liberating is indifferent to God and is theologically insignificant? If one answers in the affirmative, then one is entitled to ask: What is the *humanly and historically liberating meaning* of the function that the priests, the bishops, and the pope fulfill within the church? The validity of a theology is also measured by its concern to take up this type of questioning. On the other hand, how else is the "identity crisis" to be resolved from which the clergy is suffering (and to which we shall have to return later)? One no longer knows who one is; one cannot long endure in a task when one no longer sees the *human* and historical meaning of what one is and does and when one is obliged to resort to justifications that are at once a-historical and perversely abstract. Days are coming (and are already here) when it will no longer suffice to resort to some "will of God" in order to justify humanly insane situations.

Certainly, many things have changed. But how do matters stand with what I should call "the heart of things," the fundamental ecclesiological logic and ecclesiastical structures? It is not sufficient to speak English in order for the respective role of priests and lay people actually to break, in the celebration of the mass, for example, an alienating type of relationship with God and the sacred. In fact, *clerics will not be differently situated in the church as long as they have not ceased to resort to God as an "absolute of beginning" in order to justify the fact that they are always the absolute beginning of everything in the church.*

GOD

"To Lay People the Profane"

If clerics are entirely taken up on the side of God, lay people, for their part, are pulled entirely toward the side of the "profane." They are given, in the name of God, the gift of the world, of the "secular" world, as they say. Is this not a gift that risks sanctioning their ecclesiastical passivity in an absolute way?

While affirming their fidelity to the Second Vatican Council, the *Lineamenta*, for example, clarify the specific nature of the laity, what is proper to it and thus constitutes the original contribution of lay people in their relations to clerics: the "council presents the insertion of lay people in temporal and earthly realities, i.e. their 'secularity,' not only as a sociological datum but further and more specifically as a theological and ecclesiastical datum, as the characteristic modality according to which the Christian vocation is to be lived."[8]

At first glance, this definition is attractive. It generously entrusts to lay people a mission that is apt to arouse enthusiasm. In fact, no. 31 of *Lumen Gentium* suggests that lay people live "in the world, that is, in each and in all of the secular professions and occupations. They live in the ordinary circumstances of family and social life, from which the very web of their existence is woven. They are called there by God so that by exercising their proper function and being led by the spirit of the gospel they can work for the sanctification of the world from within, in the manner of leaven. In this way they can make Christ known to others, especially by the testimony of a life resplendent in faith, hope, and charity."

A first observation imposes itself: if this description is indeed what specifies the laity (and is thus what the clergy is not), it is implied by that very fact that the pope, the bishops, and the priests do not live in the world, that they do not have to worry about temporal things and familial and social life, in a word, that they do not have to be the leaven of the gospel in the world. Let it be said in passing that a vision of clerics is thus confirmed, today

43

A CHURCH OF THE BAPTIZED

in 1987, that forces them to leave the time of history and reaffirms that they are "men of God."

Above all, one must remember this: *lay people are entrusted with the very thing that, in the ecclesiological logic and the present structures of the church, is not God and is even experienced spontaneously as the opposite of God.*

Unless one fosters a conception of the "world" that situates it differently in the religious schema (and I shall return to this immediately), one in effect abandons to lay people what, against the background of an understanding of God as absolute transcendence, must be recognized as *the absolute bottom.* Grappling with the concrete management of conjugal and familial life which never has the clarity of the high-flown principles *concerning* the couple and the family, grappling further with social questions where the good is never perfectly separable from the bad, and engaged in a political life that never clearly expresses "the will of God," lay people thus receive the universe of *limits.* In the thought of the clerics and lay people of today, the latter therefore have as their proper domain what is contrary to an absolute transcendence, what is logically thought of and structurally identified as not being of God, and what also one is accustomed to experiencing as an obstacle that forbids being "on the side of God." Even worse (however little the mechanisms described above may be operative), the specific nature of the laity is defined from the place where a morbid and pathological guilt inevitably arises. Should one be amazed, then, that lay people constantly live their lives in the mode of a betrayal of the "official" moral standards, as an infidelity to the "church," and thus as an absolutely reprehensible infidelity since it is, in its very foundations, an infidelity to the absoluteness of God himself?

One condition was set for this perverse mechanism to come into play, namely, that the ecclesiological logic continue to be thought of in a manner that structures clergy/laity relationships as before. From this point of view, another citation of Vatican II is revealing. It expresses the responsibility of priests and invites them to a certain "generosity" in their relations with the laity. In effect, they "should listen to the laity willingly, consider their wishes in a fraternal spirit, and recognize their experience and competence in the different areas of human activity, so that together with them they will be able to read the signs of the times."[9] Immediately after, however, the priests are charged to "test the spirits (of lay people) to see if they be of God." What a responsibility! But, above all, to what really scandalous pretentiousness can the priests be invited! Do they hold the code for an existence according to the heart of God? They are not married but should know the laws that married life must follow in order to be faithful to God. They have no children, but they are asked to tell the will of God for the conduct of family life. They are a priori forbidden all social commitment, but they know the principles that should govern the common life of societies. They are also forbidden to enter into the ambiguities of political life, but they can "test the spirits" in order "to see" if the political management of worldly affairs corresponds to divine rectitude.

The absolute passivity of the laity in the structure of their relations with the clergy is thus manifested, among several other domains, by their absolute passivity in the definition of the so-called "official" *moral theology* of the church.

One will vaunt the demands of this moral theology. It only renders explicit the demands of a life that wishes to follow Jesus. One will also speak of the nobility of its vision of man and of how it speaks of a liberated humanity, one emancipated forever from all slavery. At bottom, it is all the more noble the more demanding it is. But, Fernand Dumont asks, "How can we lay people escape the impression with which we are left, manage with our problems from day to day, when the function of the clergy is to continue to repeat high-flown principles? In this fashion, a dangerous gap is opened up between the image that the official church tries to give of itself and the daily experience of Christians

A CHURCH OF THE BAPTIZED

who want to belong to the Church. One thus risks ending in a second secrecy, which is no longer that of the church at the heart of society, but a sort of 'moral poaching' within the church."[10]

This poaching, however, does not reveal the adolescent passions of persons who yield momentarily to the charms of playing truant. It challenges *the mode of constructing* the moral discourse of the church: to the clerics high-flown principles that govern the moral rectitude of Christian action; to lay people the application of the principles in the world. In effect, they have as their proper part the temporal, the quotidian and its problems, a quotidian that *never* corresponds to the purity of high-flown principles and thus *always* condemns lay people to betray the moral ideal as soon as they try to translate it. A system is thus constructed *in relation to which each person and each social body constitute an exception*—a system that really has the nature of ideology and plays on persons and collectivities as an absolute authority that judges them and makes them feel guilty.

Confronted with the drama of certain lives, several clerics see well that it is pastorally necessary to propose something else. They then give evidence of an exceptional "openness," as is often said. But do they see that they are just demonstrating the perverse abstraction of high-flown principles and of the so-called "official" moral discourse? They will be merciful toward the divorced and remarried, but without being able to permit them access to eucharistic communion; one should love homosexual persons but condemn their acts, etc.

The price to be paid for the elaboration and the maintenance of the official moral discourse is a heavy one since the latter is only constructed thanks to a separation between *being* and *acting*, a dichotomization of both personal and collective existence. This dichotomy relies on another separation, that lived in clergy/laity relationships, at the same time that it nourishes it. There is, on the one side, being, the high-flown principles, and the clerics who "know" being, define the high-flown principles,

46

GOD

and take charge of repeating them. The other side is that of historical action, of ambiguities, and lay people who have no other responsibility than that of executing what has been decided and defined by others, by the clerics: "It is as if, today as always, one affirmed that the diagnosis to be made of problems, doctrine, and moral standards was exclusively a matter for the priests, the bishops, and the pope and that we have in no way to meddle with it. *You lay people,* we are made to understand, *are executors: we charge you with converting those whom we cannot reach. You have your word to say about practical things and about the questions that do not touch on what is essential to Christianity.*"[11]

The clergy thus entrusts to lay people the execution of principles in profane and secular history. But since history is the place of limits, for lack of being able to translate them, lay people betray them. There is evidently a logical and structural defect here: if the only responsibility of lay people is one of betrayal, is it not because they have first been refused every role as an active subject in the formulation of the principles and in the *construction* of the moral discourse? In the end, this passivity is only a particular form of a generalized passivity, that of the laity in its relationships with the clergy and the whole of ecclesiastical life.

3.   Opening the Ecclesiastical Future of Lay People

As soon as God, or the idea of God, or relations to God, or language about God is mentioned, one knows more or less confusedly that he or she is touching on fundamental realities. These realities are not immediately grasped in themselves, even if they are immediately decisive for the conduct of life. One senses challenges that are not so much of the nature of the *calculable future*, of what has to be projected today onto tomorrow or the day after. Yet, their formulation cannot be abandoned to the imagination of the futurologists. More than the calculable future (but without denying the importance that should be accorded to

47

A CHURCH OF THE BAPTIZED

it), more than tomorrow or the day after, the evocation of God invites one to think of the *open future*, i.e. the dimension of *openness* of the today that we are living.

From this perspective, the task is not now to draft a little catechism, a catalogue of "things to do," and even less to propose recipes that will guarantee a correct result. If I propose *four challenges*, it is because I believe them to be unavoidable and eminently practical if there is to be an openness to the future of the laity. These challenges will not, however, be explicit in their Christian and christological implications. I wish, above all, to formulate questions which will be discussed in the next chapter whose focus is on Jesus Christ.

Learning To Name God

If one listens to the vocabulary that is employed to say "God," one can ask oneself what is truly "Christian" about these images.[12] It is, furthermore, striking to notice how some, in public prayer, for example, address themselves to *God*, to the *good Lord*, to the *Father*, to the *Holy Spirit*, to *Jesus*, to the *all-powerful*, etc., as if all these terms covered the same reality, and without knowing too well if each one refers to a specific type of relationship with God.

A troubling question that each one can and should address to oneself is: How is my faith in Jesus Christ expressed in my spontaneous visions of God? Can I truly make this saying my motto: "I know no other God than the God *of Jesus Christ*"? Jesus Christ has indeed died and risen for some purpose, "in order to save us," we say, in order to have us die to death and to permit our entry into life. What does that say about God or about our images of God? Or should one not hear there a call to *die* to certain images of God that are ultimately fatal? Henri Bourgeois affirms: "We live in an epoch in which the name of God sometimes grows dark and becomes problematic. It thus belongs to christology not to let the Christian faith be reduced to a theism. It

48

falls to it to pose the question of God in a historically determinate manner, on the basis of Jesus and in view of Jesus."[13] "I am the way, the truth, and the life." Does this statement not mean, in particular, that no one enters into the truth of God outside this *way* that is Jesus Christ? A first challenge is thus that *Christian believers must learn again and again to* name *their God as the God of "Jesus Christ."*

The institutional passivity of the laity finds its first and last reason in a certain image of God, in the historically alienated relation that this image reflects and nourishes.[14] It would be as well to affirm that without a conversion of this vision of God, the laity has no future. Does the confession of Jesus Christ as liberator permit one to be liberated from this perverse God, the words that describe him, and the relation in which he is destroying human freedom? The Christian faith confesses that Jesus Christ instituted new and liberating relations to God. It is again necessary to learn them and to name them unceasingly *in* life and *from* the existence, which is always more or less free, that men and women are living.

Once again, a reality as historical and concrete as the open future of the laity is at stake. In fact, only the act of trying to name God ("God is the God *of Jesus Christ*") will emancipate lay people from the hold of persons and groups that appropriate God for themselves, make themselves the guarantors of his truth, and try to impose it on others. Only this permits one to escape from the domination of clerics insofar as clerics claim to be the sole active subjects of a relation and arrogate to themselves the truth of this relation because they have first identified their own truth as the truth "of God." From this point of view, that ambition is short-sighted which limits itself to wanting immediately to transform the ecclesiastical status and the behavior patterns of those who today are identified as being of the clergy. Without the detour through the questions about God, the odds are that one will favor the emergence of other clerics, "men of God," who will claim to

A CHURCH OF THE BAPTIZED

be directly united to God and who, without being the old clerics, will just as much arrogate to themselves the right to maintain others in an absolute passivity.

Situating Oneself on the Side of God

Lay people see themselves assigned the status of a passive object by a game that keeps them at a distance from God. This dynamic removes God, forces his retreat behind an absolute transcendence that seems to be unrelated to the march of history. It thus wishes to safeguard God as the absolute beginning of all, but it actually erects him into an absolute authority that makes people feel guilty and, far from always commencing their liberation, alienates them absolutely. Why does this game destroy human freedom? History is the place where human beings grapple with the limits of what is called "the world." Can history then be situated anywhere else than opposite from God and be anything other than God's radical *contrary?*

Furthermore, this is what was entrusted to lay people as their proper domain; it is the profaneness of the world that specifies their ecclesiastical status. It would be as well to say that they have learned to situate themselves opposite from God, separated from him by that which is his contrary (the limits of the world) and which defines them. To formulate a second challenge, *lay people will not forsake their status as a passive object if it is impossible for them to be situated on the side of God.*

As long as lay people give themselves the world (or it is entrusted to them, without realizing that it is a poisoned gift) as the defining element of their being and their mission, they are forced to live the limits of history as an obstacle that is placed between them and God. Lay people, however, do not have the leisure of leaving history because it is their proper place, the very thing that defines them ecclesiastically. They are thus launched upon a quest that is a priori desperate and hopeless. Like the carrot before the nose of the ass, God is removed from them whenever they approach him. Once a given challenge is taken up, once certain limits are overcome, others arise which move God a little farther away. Because of history, human beings will never be finished struggling with the limits of their world. If lay people cannot situate themselves on the side of God, their quest for him will thus condemn them, concretely speaking, to an endless frustration which has no exit in time and history.

As "men of God," entirely taken up on his side, clerics have become distant and strange. For a long time they have learned to situate themselves opposite lay people, and that is where one wants to keep them when they try to draw closer. For their part, and because they always grapple with the universe of limits, lay people have no other choice than to stand *opposite the clergy*, far away from them, forced to make them the reference for life "according to God." But if they are authorized to situate themselves "on the side of God" and thus to reverse the dynamic of their relationship with him, they are only forsaking their ontological status, so to speak, as a passive object. In principle (*in principio:* in the principle itself that can inaugurate something else), *they have become capable of radically subverting their relationship with the clerics.* For this relationship can evidently no longer be from the clergy to the laity, from subject to object. In doing so, would they not demonstrate the inanity of the present ecclesiastical structure, of the organization of clergy/laity relationships as it is structured today? Is it still justifiable to speak of "lay people" and of "clerics" if one recognizes the possibility of belief in a God who has taken everything "onto his side"? One begins to dream. . . .

Called To Experience God in History

Some dreams alienate. Others liberate, insofar as they eliminate pride and set in motion an historical work of liberation. It is nice to believe that humanity is already on the side of God. This claim, however, is itself fatal if, in order to live on the side of

A CHURCH OF THE BAPTIZED

God, men and women must be exiled from the side of history. In order for lay people to effect a change in their relations to God and to escape from passivity (and from the hold of the clerics), they must be able to say: *it is "here and now" that human beings can be on the side of God.*

To deplore the remoteness of the God of the customary visions was, in short, to formulate the necessity of a God who is near and dwells in a history that is the natural habitat of humanity. This personal and collective history poses the challenge of liberation and of the tasks that must be assumed for the history of freedom to be written. By seeking life with God elsewhere, in some ethereal heaven without historical substance, men and women cease to be the subject of their history.

During the absence of some of humanity from history, the human species has not ceased to make the necessary historical transformations and to express the urgency of human tasks. But the exile into God has concretely paralyzed many. And it is God, or more precisely their vision of God, that is the cause of this alienation. In effect, their flight and the abandonment of their responsibilities have concretely submitted them to the designs of powers that, during the time of their exile, shape history according to their own interests. It is not surprising that believers then find themselves in a world that they do not recognize, of which they now feel themselves to be slaves. The laity cannot achieve the status of an active subject *if history and its limits have not become the obligatory place of a true encounter with God, the sole place of life in God, of responsibility and activity.*

If the place of meeting with God is thus displaced, the relationships of lay people with the clergy inevitably become different. Lay people evidently cannot put up with attitudes and patterns of behavior that continue to make the clergy strange and distant. But the question is more radical. It leaves the level of attitudes and patterns of behavior and challenges *the very possibility of a clergy that is the sole active subject.* If lay people were

GOD

defined by the negative, they were nothing ecclesiastically. If they now claim to be on the side of God and are called to be so in the very place that was formerly considered the bottom, is there still a "bottom" that remains and a "top" that would specify the place of the clerics? The present structure of clergy/laity relations has lost its justification. The two terms have, in effect, disappeared *as they were understood and as they were made to enter into the dynamics of the relation.*

The Existence of God and Human Decision

The two last points permit us to go further. The status of passive object finds its *raison d'être* in the absolute passivity of all that is situated in the schema below God. It is nice to affirm, in order to heal this passivity, the possibility of now being on the side of God, of making clear that such a proximity is lived here and now, and of concluding to a marriage of God and of history. But how does God intervene in history through believers, and how do believers make their world enter into the gratuitous freedom of God? Without an answer to this question, the old dichotomizing logic may well be displaced while still remaining intact. This time it will be operative *within believing conscious-nesses,* and the latter will more than ever be the victims of perverse structures.

How are the relationships between the *faith* of believers and their human *history* to be conceived? One thing is certain: historical existence cannot be seen as a passage that would only go from faith *toward* history. And nevertheless, certain understandings of faith, certain ways of living it, give one to understand that it constitutes a universe in itself where the truth of God resides, from which the true nature of history can be drawn, and *from which* one can then go to work on a transformation of the world that would express the will of God for the world.

But when believers confront the ambiguities of the world, they no longer know very well the historical form that the truth

53

A CHURCH OF THE BAPTIZED

supposedly pre-defined in their faith should take. If they have ceased to be torn between two exterior poles (God and the world), it is within their consciousness that the dichotomy now operates, within themselves that they experience the tear. Only two possible ways stand open: either the world is absolutely impervious to divine life, and the only possibility is to take refuge in faith as a capacity for finding God directly; or the passage from God to the world is effected immediately, without mediation, where the direct intervention of God is always made in the mode of the miraculous. In both cases, *human freedom* is held in contempt. It does not have to intervene since it could only muddle the immediacy of the relationships between God and the world. That is why, when indicating the place of God in the deductive schema, I spoke of him as an absolute beginning, but specified that he is seen above all as an *absolute of beginning:* God would always begin to intervene immediately, without human liberty being able to decide anything at all. One thus does not forsake the exclusively deductive logic if it is impossible to confess that *God exists in history when persons and collectivities humanly decide to make him exist.* Let us be more precise: in decisions that, by definition, are never clinically pure. No other god is worthy of human beings because such a god would presuppose a human being that is not worthy of God.

Such a respect for human decision does not deny the gratuitousness of God. It is even necessary in order for this gratuitousness to be respected *as* gratuitousness and for God to be respected as God. This question is so fundamental that the fate of all anthropology is at stake here. I should say only that one gains some idea of its importance from the repercussions that are felt on the ecclesiastical status of clerics and lay people. If lay people can place their faith in God *in* their human decisions, they cease to conceive his action as a direct intervention in history, and their humanity becomes necessary for God's existence in the world.

54

GOD

How could they consent to continue to live a relation in which the clergy is everything and they are nothing?

At first glance, the question of God seems to be indifferent for the concrete fate of lay people. On closer examination, however, one notices that it is absolutely necessary to return to it if one wants to free the present and open up the future of the laity. The actual structure of clergy/laity relationships defines each term in such a way that, in order for the structure to be converted and the relationships of subject to object to disappear, the terms themselves must disappear. The future of the laity is that it may disappear. May a people of believers arise who will form relations of faith among themselves for which all will be humanly responsible personally and communally.

3

(Jesus) Christ

Mediator between God and Men

After God comes Christ. He constitutes the second element in the schema, which gives the impression that he is understood, one could say, against the background of God. But is he situated as God is situated? No doubt, our heritage is very coherent. It can be presumed that the religious mentality proposes a structure of life and of rigorous thought, a structure from which none of the elements escape. It is thus legitimate to ask oneself if the deductive logic has been operative in our understanding of Jesus Christ and if, speaking now of him whom we confess as savior, an *active top* and a *passive bottom* was set up.

If one maintains relations with him in which human freedom is condemned to passivity (and let us note in passing that there is then a contradiction in terms), the God of our spontaneous visions does not succeed in being mediated in history. To speak now of Jesus Christ is thus to ask oneself about his mediation. Christians confess him as the *only mediator between God and men*. But there is often a distance between explicit confession and the structures of thought and life. Furthermore, theology evidently cannot explain the mediation of Jesus Christ: the latter reflects too much the mystery of his person; it is irreducible to a concept and even to any system that wishes to give coherence to a set of concepts. But theology can at least try to pose the right questions and, above all, to situate the questioning in the place that the mediation of Jesus suggests.

Where and how does the Christian question concerning Christ the mediator arise? This is an immense subject which calls for a reflection on the whole of the christological mystery and to which it is thus impossible to do full justice within the limits of the present work. But one can begin to meet the challenge if one remembers the particular objective being pursued: verifying the hypothesis according to which the Christian religious mentality (in this case, our vision of Christ and of our relations to him) answered to and still answers to an *exclusively deductive* movement. The pursuit of this objective will respect the three moments already established in the preceding chapter: after having described the heritage, we shall say how it takes form in the structure of clergy/laity relations, and then open up some ways to the future of the laity.

1. A Theistic Vision Even of Jesus Christ?

The title of this chapter places one term (*Jesus*) in parentheses. This placing in parentheses is deliberate. At first glance, it suggests that our heritage has exhausted the *entire* mystery of Jesus Christ in the second term, *Christ*. The Christian confession reflects a complex reality in which two terms (*Jesus* and *Christ*) are both equally essential. This fact already expresses a demand, for a relationship with Jesus Christ that is correct from a Christian point of view requires of believers that they fully respect his divinity *and* his humanity at one and the same time. Furthermore, it does not suffice to affirm the two poles as if they only rubbed shoulders. What are their *relationships?* What type of *relation* do they maintain?

My hypothesis is that this relation has essentially been thought of in the mode of physical causality. In doing so, it is *within the person of Jesus Christ* that a dichotomizing caesura has been effected which locks up the humanity and the divinity of Jesus Christ in two worlds so that it is hard to see how they are reconciled, two worlds that ultimately end by appearing contrary

A CHURCH OF THE BAPTIZED

and contradictory. I should say more precisely that the divinity of
Jesus Christ has been understood as a *top* where he is realized as a
subject of salvation and as a *bottom*, his humanity being a *passive
object* submitted to the plan of salvation that God nourished for
humanity from all eternity. Bernard Sesboué comes close to the
question I am posing: "It was far from being certain, however,
that this current, which had been led to see only God in Jesus and
to underestimate the authentic man, had not reached us by
multiple channels. Preaching is always the reflection of the theology of a period, and that which formed what is called 'classical'
Catholicism was marked to a greater or lesser degree by a 'mono-
physite' tendency, i.e., as we have just seen, a tendency which
retains only the divine nature of Christ."[1]

The Christ of Glory

The common perception wants the "real truth" of Jesus Christ
to be unfolded in the field of his divinity and there alone. To say
"Jesus Christ" is identical to saying "God." Spontaneous prayer, as
I have just indicated, reflects well this identification that reduces
the entire personal mystery to a single one of its defining elements:
one addresses oneself indifferently to God or to Jesus while aiming
at one and the same undifferentiated reality.

The idea commonly formed of the *consciousness* of Jesus is
particularly revealing of the present structure of the Christian
mentality. It also unfortunately expresses an inability to see his
humanity otherwise than as something insignificant, an object
submitted to the dictates of the divinity. It is necessary to add that
theological discourses have hardly helped. Too many of them
still reject the fact a priori that the consciousness of Jesus was
submitted to the laws of every human consciousness, that it was a
truly *historical* reality, and thus obliged to undergo a journey,
being confronted by limits, ambiguity, temptation, and doubt.
"Traditional christology," writes Bruno Forte, understands "the
consciousness of Jesus in terms of a descending schema. . . . It

(JESUS) CHRIST

derived from it the image of an 'omniscient' Jesus, one constantly in the presence of the contemplation of God in beatitude."[2] The Christian people has thus learned to "divinize" the consciousness of Jesus, to make of it a place of *immediacy*, of direct and constant contact with God. And this divinization was to take place as soon as possible, from the womb of Mary, his mother.

The consequences of such ventures still make themselves cruelly felt. They have accustomed us to place the meaning of salvation outside the humanity of Jesus Christ, the latter becoming a sort of salvifically insignificant parenthesis. In doing so, one confers on Jesus a role that, through lack of taking the incarnation and its laws seriously, withdraws his mediation from history. He becomes distant and seems to live in human history without committing himself much to it, to make his way there while already knowing exactly the point of arrival, and to struggle with absolute foresight of a final victory. He advances sovereignly toward his death without experiencing in his flesh the implacable laws of death, for he "knows" the resurrection, that it alone counts, that it is thus *unrelated* to death and the density it has as an historical fact. For traditional theology, Bruno Forte writes again, "it was through condescendence to humanity and with a pedagogical aim that Jesus played the role of one who was ignorant of some things: his human condition was a 'parody of humanity.' "[3] Are they wrong who reject such a Jesus and find that it constitutes the worst contempt ever shown to human freedom? It is the worst because it provides itself with an absolute justification in a certain understanding of the divinity of Jesus and thus of God.

At bottom, our heritage has privileged two moments in the existence of Jesus Christ: first, the incarnation, the descent of God into human history; then, the return to God at the resurrection. The period in between is without interest since Jesus is seen to lead an "exemplary" life there. But that just reduces the human life of Jesus Christ to the function of an example or a

59

A CHURCH OF THE BAPTIZED

model. Jesus becomes the "sublime example"—all that but nothing else. Why have the christological works of F.-X. Durwell, which were not published very long ago, seemed so liberating?[4] By reducing the personal mystery of Jesus Christ to his divinity, one had got used to assimilating *Easter* and *resurrection*, the two terms being equivalent and, in short, offering an identical content. The intention of Durwell is to break with these customary visions; he speaks of Easter as the death-resurrection. The death of Jesus (and, in an inevitable backward movement, his entire historical existence) thus become part of the paschal mystery. From the Christian point of view, his death is essential in the (minimal) sense that the divinity of Jesus Christ cannot be correctly situated *outside its ties* to his humanity and the concrete history of this concrete man.

The divinity of Christ alone counted; it alone was the subject of a salvation, one could say, that the humanity of Jesus passively accompanied, that it underwent. Paradoxically perhaps, this dichotomy is confirmed by the slight place (or the absence) of the Spirit in the general mentality and the discourse of the churches of the west. In scarcely the last few years, the latter have experienced a remarkable, sudden appearance of the Spirit, or, rather, an explosion of words about the Spirit. One was so little accustomed to this that life and reflection were caught unawares. On the one hand, theology realized the poverty of its pneumatological discourse, its abstraction, and the slight interest it presented for the conduct of Christian and ecclesiastical life. Even worse, all fields of reflection (christology, ecclesiology, etc.) had lost the concern to take account, each field in turn, of the place and function of the Spirit of Jesus Christ. As a result, believers found themselves lacking, incapable of naming the Spirit, who they said was alive, and of identifying it as the Spirit *of Jesus Christ*. It quickly became evident, in effect, that many drew the Spirit entirely to the side of the miraculous, assimilated it to the extraordinary, the unusual; the Spirit was so ineffable that it

(JESUS) CHRIST

meant everything, no matter what, and in the end nothing. "When one no longer knows how to be," writes Jean Duché, "pretenses help one to live, the unusual reassures."[5]

How does this phenomenon constitute a supplementary support for the hypothesis according to which the person of Jesus Christ was understood according to only one pole, that of his divinity? The virtual ignorance of what was situated at the bottom (i.e. the humanity of Jesus and the role of history in his personal consciousness) prevented seeing how the Spirit first had to intervene in the existence *of Jesus himself.* For all practical purposes, Jesus was identified with God, and one may well ask why the Spirit would have been necessary for the accomplishment of his being and his mission. The New Testament has Jesus say that his departure is "to our advantage" and that the advantage consists precisely in the fact that the departure of Jesus will assure the "gift of the Spirit." But how can this gift be to our advantage if it is not first so for Jesus? Everything is connected: without the christological foundations of a life in the Spirit, Christian anthropology was itself poorly prepared to respect the place that falls to the Spirit in the historical conduct of our lives. Once one had ceased seeing the ties of the Spirit to the humanity of Jesus (which is inevitable when one approaches his mystery only by way of his divinity), it was impossible to assure his marriage with history, with our history. Distortions of existence, odd patterns of behavior, and inacceptable exaggerations of language follow from this.

The Humanity of Jesus and His Mediation of Salvation

In the meantime, what becomes of the humanity pole? When the entire meaning of mediation has gone to take refuge on the side of the divinity, does not the saving action escape from the man who is Jesus, or, more precisely, from what should constitute him as a true human being: his freedom and capacity for decision? The history of Jesus becomes, in effect, the long account of a passive submission—submission to God, but, still

61

A CHURCH OF THE BAPTIZED

more directly, submission of his humanity to the God that he himself is!

One continues, of course, to speak of the humanity of Jesus Christ. How could one dare to call oneself a Christian if, with one's gaze resting on Jesus Christ, one closes the entire field of his humanity and of his history? The debarment of the first pole does not render the second one mute. On the contrary, however paradoxical it may seem, discourses become all the more numerous and eloquent as the entire truth of Jesus Christ is supposed to be exhausted in his divinity. Is one ever more eloquent than when one comes to the defense of a desperate cause? It does not, however, suffice to speak of a reality in order to assure that it is situated in a way that is valid from a Christian point of view. It is necessary to ask oneself again: *How*, then, does one speak of the humanity of Jesus, and, above all, how is it situated in the inviolable dynamics of Christian salvation? Even more precisely, in the act of mediation of Jesus Christ, how does one understand the *relations* of his humanity to his divinity?

This is evidently an immense question. Has christology ever confronted any other questions than this one? Here the ambition is modest and asks only what becomes of the humanity of Jesus when the entire mystery has fled to the side of his divinity. Springing from religious mentalities that it nourishes in return, language slides over two apparently divergent slopes. Popular wisdom and philosophy observe that contraries are of the same genus, and this surprising encounter of contraries is in fact confirmed by the language that is commonly employed to express the humanity of Jesus. Two types of relationships with the texts of the New Testament may, in particular, illustrate these two slidings of language and of mentality.

1. The first relationship would merit as precise an analysis as possible because it sometimes assumes such refined forms that it is possible to enter into its movement without even perceiving it. But the fate that it reserves for the humanity of Jesus is too

(JESUS) CHRIST

clear for it to be necessary to insist very long upon it. A gaze is made to rest on the humanity of Jesus, a return is effected to his history, to what he was, said, and did. But, in the end, the return has only the objective of *passing directly to his divinity*. Practically speaking, his humanity only serves as a pretext. One resorts to the sayings and deeds of Jesus, but these are only a support of which faith makes use in order to forsake it immediately, to leap elsewhere, to soar upward toward the true world, that which counts from the point of view of salvation and of mediation, which is the world of his divinity.[6]

This procedure does not hide its presuppositions very well. Such a relationship with the history of Jesus is not, in fact, possible unless God himself intervenes directly in each deed and each word, at every moment of the life of Jesus, and divinizes in some way each of his words and each of his deeds. The action of God appears sovereign, capable of a constant "introjection." Thanks to this, it takes at every instant the initiative of giving to the life, words, and deeds of Jesus a meaning entirely different from that which he is humanly capable of deciding. In spite of the fact that his words remain human words, we are given to understand, one should not stop at them and focus one's attention on their surface human meaning since each one is only an occasion for God directly to reveal his salvation. One thus lapses into a relationship with Jesus in which everything is miraculous and each word and each deed operate miraculously. It would be as well to say that the humanity of Jesus is salvifically insignificant. What he was able to decide as a human being, what he thought, experienced, and said, the history of his personal freedom, and his own integration into the history of his people—all that is only a *passive object* entirely delivered up to a direct intervention of God.

One limit experience crystallizes, as it were, the activity of God and the passivity of the man Jesus, and that is the *resurrection*. How, from these perspectives, can one read it otherwise

63

A CHURCH OF THE BAPTIZED

than as the miracle *par excellence,* an absolute accomplishment of the miraculous? It is simply an occasion for God to take possession of another limit experience, that of death, and to breathe into it a meaning that is its very *opposite,* a meaning of life. That is no doubt why what was said earlier about the paschal mystery was rendered possible: the entire positive content of Easter was understood from only one of the two poles, the resurrection. Nevertheless, one cannot help noticing that, if the resurrection thus absolutely accomplishes the sovereign action of God, it equally sanctions the sovereign passivity of the man Jesus.

Nothing is changed in the problem if it is specified that this acting God is in Jesus, that Jesus is God. Such a statement only succeeds in radicalizing a dichotomy that now effects a scission within the person of Jesus Christ. It is in his being that there is henceforth a radical separation of the divine and of the human. It would be as well to say that the confession of the mediation no longer has any meaning. It falls into the absurd. And if the Christian faith condemns us to paradox, we may never use it to justify absurdity. On the one hand, one would confess Jesus Christ as the only mediator between God and men at the same time that, from another side, the meaning of salvation escapes from his humanity by the absolute separation that has been presupposed. In fact, such a mediator does not mediate anything.

2. Let us pass over to a second type of religious mentality that is frequently encountered. The relationship with the humanity of Jesus here takes on a direction that seems quite opposed to the first. Far from reducing the historicity of Jesus to a pretext that permits it to flee elsewhere, faith is engulfed, as it were, in the density of brute and objectified facts, or, more specifically, of facts that in and through their historicity would immediately express salvation in a way that would thus be confining for human understanding. If certain ones, be it understood, do not believe in Jesus Christ as mediator of a universal salvation, it is because they are resisting the "evidence of facts." The words and deeds inscribed in the New

(JESUS) CHRIST

Testament are no longer pretexts for going elsewhere. Every deed, on the contrary, deserves that one rest in its brute facticity, for the latter has become a bearer of an immediately given meaning of salvation. And every word that Jesus said becomes, as a humanly evident fact, a "word of salvation."

This second mentality, in turn, does not hide very well a considerable presupposition: the relationships that it establishes between human facts and mediation suppose that one has first considered history as a place where salvation can be received as a brute datum, so to speak, an historically evident fact. It is in this that the extreme fragility of certain Christians resides. Such a relationship with the history of Jesus effectively leaves the Christian consciousness quite disarmed before historical criticism (and recent history should have taught us a lot about that). An equivalence has been set up thanks to which the divinity of Jesus has come to be identified with words and to be lost in definite facts and deeds. It thus suffices passively to *receive* the history of Jesus, what his human deeds and words mean, in order to enter into the dynamics of his salvific mediation. In the end, we would be the passive object of a past that always pre-contains the truth of the present.

But the contemporary understanding sets up different relationships with the past and with past facts. It has quite correctly demonstrated that no one (not even a professional historian) can content himself or herself with going back with the simple gathering of factual data as an objective. In the more particular area of faith, the believing consciousness is discovering more and more that things of the past, scripture in particular, express and illuminate the faith on the condition that this be the faith of today, a faith that is always historically situated and that takes the initiative of going to question them. Is that not what liberation theology, for example, is teaching us?

The second relationship thus constitutes a second way of canonizing our passivity, so to speak, since human understanding

65

A CHURCH OF THE BAPTIZED

has only to submit to the evidence of salvation that the words and deeds immediately yield. One lauds a return to the past but in the hope of finding there someone who will clearly, *and thus immediately*, express salvation. No distance (which would nevertheless clear a space for faith) has been introduced, or at least it is no longer fostered, between the words and their meaning of salvation. The mediation of Jesus Christ is paralyzed a second time, his divinity having come to be lost in brute facticity.

Exegetes put us on guard against a recourse to scripture that too easily follows the bent of this second movement. But in spite of the fact that Christian persons and communities are now more informed of the dangers of such a fundamentalism, do we still escape the fatal seductions of its logic? I am not certain of it. One has only to see the constant resurgence of attempts that present Jesus as a *model* and the Christian life as a *value* or a *system of values*. Nothing is changed in this matter if one qualifies this model that Jesus is supposed to be as "sublime," just as the problem we have indicated has not been left once values have been baptized and are spoken of as "Christian" values. If every value is a creation of human freedom, Jesus Christ (and salvation) have been reduced to being only one element among several in the *homogeneous* universe of values.

Here the death of Jesus constitutes a limit experience. It would be necessary to speak of it at length, but it will suffice to recall the place that it occupies in the religious mentality. Humanly speaking, does it mean anything else in its brute character as a fact than a period? It marks the term of a life, it closes the book of a human existence. It is thus felt by the believing consciousness as a non-sense, the absolute non-sense and the absolute *opposite* of life. In order to overcome this non-sense, and because it is necessary to express the victory of the resurrection, what other way is there than that of a moralizing spiritualization? Jesus dies, but it is a quite exemplary death, worse than all others, and *that is why* the resurrection takes on its depth. There is no

66

(JESUS) CHRIST

need at all to insist on it: so many spiritualities have been constructed that have exalted death in a morbid way and have lauded sufferings, those anticipated deaths, as an end in themselves and as desirable since they permit one to draw near to an exemplary death, that of Jesus. How, then, can the final abandonment of Jesus be read otherwise than as a passive submission to a supremely tyrannical will of God? How can it be received as a sovereignly free human act, freer than any act that can be imagined? Submitted to facticity, and thus incapable of situating the resurrection (which is irreducible to the facticity of an object of history) *in* what Jesus is living, consciousness has lost Jesus Christ and has lost itself in a sort of dehumanizing masochism.

The problem, of course, is one of understanding the faith, and it raises important epistemological questions. But it is not only posed for the specialists in reflection. On the contrary! How many Christians are still profoundly troubled today as soon as a reading of scripture is proposed to them that does not take at face value a relationship of immediacy between human words and their meaning of salvation? And how many say they have lost their faith when, having ceased to be credulous, they have decided no longer to abandon the meaning of their lives into the hands of a model who, at the bar of human understanding and of a greater awakening to history, finally appears to them as being in effect only one model among several others, which occasions the traumatisms to which freedom is always submitted when it lets itself be defined by the ideal of a model?

Why is there this "loss of faith" when the words and deeds attributed to Jesus are passed through the sieve of historical criticism, when he has ceased to be the sublime example, or when, in a world turned upside down, the values that were called "Christian" have collapsed at the same time as all others? Once again, it is because one has presupposed, without always being conscious of it, an *immediacy* between the divinity of Jesus Christ and his humanity, an immediacy that alone can allow human words to

67

A CHURCH OF THE BAPTIZED

yield directly a meaning of salvation. One probably wished to do justice to the incarnation and the history of Jesus, to restore to Jesus Christ the freedom of a true man, one capable of decision, and to respect him as an active human subject. But that point was only reached at the price of a *concrete negation of his mediation*: human decision is really no longer possible when it is supposed that God intervenes immediately and that history is read as the simple and immediate transcription of a plan of salvation. The freedom of the man Jesus has thus been *objectified* and sovereignly submitted to passivity.

And this is how the two contraries are of the same genus: these two relationships with the humanity of Jesus end in the same result since both sanction the *passivity* of Jesus Christ and prevent his really being the historical mediator of salvation. On the other hand, this paralysis of mediation is produced in virtue of a *defect* that is *common* to the two approaches: one of the two poles to be reconciled (the historical humanity) escapes from Jesus Christ in the concrete. It does not enter as an essential and "defining" element in the understanding of the mediator as an *agent of salvation.*

The Christian faith has (and will probably always have) to resist those views that dichotomize the person of Jesus Christ, be it by losing his humanity in an a-historical divinity, be it by burying his divinity in the history of a man whose human freedom would thus become really insignificant from the point of view of salvation. The name itself (Jesus Christ) indicates a complexity and demands a double refusal at the very least: no *Jesus* without the *Christ* and vice versa. Since it is a question of *one* double refusal, the place of the christological mystery is specified: not in one pole *or* the other, not in Jesus *or* the Christ, but in the in-between, that terrible blank space that expresses the Christian fragility and originality at the same time. The French language, as does English, tends to eliminate the hyphen that was

68

introduced between "Jesus" and "Christ" to express the name of the mediator "Jesus Christ." Personally, I see something there other than literary caprice. The hyphen, in effect, invites one to too hasty reconciliations; it favors laziness (intellectual or other) by saying too quickly that one and the same person accomplishes the encounter of humanity and divinity, whereas the blank space reveals the fragility of faith because it can be perceived as a void and always opens the possibility of ventures that dichotomize and rend existence. But it also indicates the originality of our confession insofar as the God of Christians wishes to slip in there and express the radical newness of his marriage with history. *The field of Christian existence is thus unfolded there.*

That is why, personally, I should pose a sort of preliminary question to the specialists in christology: Is it really there, in this particular blank space, that your reflection is at work? It is our ways of inhabiting this space that will perhaps help believers to foil all the ventures that try to rend the inviolable unity of an historical existence.

2. To the Clerics Christ, to Lay People the Incarnation

In addition to these considerations on the way in which the Christian mentality has become used to perceiving the divinity and the humanity of Jesus Christ, one can ask oneself: Do not Christians today have a theistic vision even of Jesus Christ? Raymond Winkling addresses this reproach to "classical theology" which, according to him, "claimed to be able to furnish explanations by adopting the point of view of God. In doing so, one had the tendency to forget the decisive value of Jesus' life of humble obedience: the humanity of Jesus was blurred in favor of a christology that, by placing the accent on his divinity, did not always escape subtle forms of docetism."[7] If clergy/laity relations are so strained today, if violence is even being done to

A CHURCH OF THE BAPTIZED

lay people in order that they may remain in their passivity, is it not because the ecclesiastical structure concretely reproduces this theism and because it is the "sacrament," as it were, of the dichotomy that disfigures Jesus Christ the mediator? The church is organized today in such a way that, in order to justify its structural defects, it must resort to a christology that separates what is united in Jesus Christ. The organization, in return, reinforces and maintains this christology. And, in the last analysis, that is the cause of our sadness in the face of the present structures and the reason that mobilizes the energies for a conversion of clergy/laity relationships.

The next chapter will explicitly analyze the theology of the *priest-mediator*, that "other Christ," as one used to say, an expression that has become current and that indicates well what pole of the mystery clerics have appropriated for themselves (or which has been given to them as their proper domain). It will then be possible to name a bit better, this time from the clerics, the christological distortions on which the ecclesiological logic and the ecclesiastical structures that we have inherited rely. For the moment, it will suffice to verify how we always have the ecclesiological vision that our christology deserves. A brief look at the conciliar decree on *The Ministry and Life of Priests* will illustrate this decisive function of the christological foundations. Yet it must be a look that is not fixed only on the final product, the decree itself (December 1965), but one that evokes its genesis and its movement by comparing it to the first, somewhat inconsistent draft, *Document IV* (November 1964).[8]

1. All commentators agree in recognizing the revolutionary newness of the approach taken by Vatican II in situating the ecclesiastical place of priests and bishops. Certainly, great ambiguities remain, but they seem normal as soon as the decree is situated in the perspective of the long history. It is nevertheless clear that the council declericalized the vocabulary that expressed the presbyterate and the episcopate. It is a declericalization that

70

(JESUS) CHRIST

goes further, that affects the theology even more than the words. The change experienced by the council fathers can be expressed in the following way: in *Document IV* the priests have the *power* to "offer visibly . . . the unbloody sacrifice of Christ," whereas in the final draft they have become *servants*, their *ministry* being understood as a *diaconal function* that can only be expressed correctly by a terminology that forsakes the vocabulary of power and assumes that of service.

But what christological foundations permit this change from power to service? Do the priests remain "men of God" who keep the lay people below in tutelage? Are they the holders of an immediacy with Christ, as the unfortunate habit of John Paul II of writing to the priests on Holy Thursday would have it understood? According to him, the "priesthood" of priests springs from Holy Thursday, from a Holy Thursday seen as the feast of a warmth which resembles a fusion and which would render priests much "closer" to the heart of Jesus than simple lay persons.[9]

In effect, there is in the movement of conciliar thought a radical change of christological foundations. I note first that the final draft makes no allusion to Holy Thursday. But furthermore, in *Document IV*, the priests' power is transmitted to them directly by *the glorious Christ:* "But when by his ascension he was taken from their eyes, our pontiff, seated invisibly at the right hand of the Father, wished nonetheless to exercise his eternal priesthood visibly in the church on earth and to make manifest his own action. That is why he consecrated to himself in a particular fashion by the anointing of the Spirit 'certain faithful' who would be able 'to act in his own name.' " *The Ministry and Life of Priests* radically displaces these christological justifications. It no longer ties the priesthood of priests directly to the Christ of glory but rediscovers history and inscribes the ministry in the wake of the *incarnation:* "So it was that Christ sent the apostles just as he himself had been sent by the Father. Through these same apos-

71

A CHURCH OF THE BAPTIZED

tles he made their successors, the bishops, sharers in his consecration and mission. Their ministerial role has been handed down to priests in a limited degree" (no. 2).

Can one be sensitive to such fundamental slidings when one only reads the final draft of the conciliar texts? This final draft, let us repeat, conveys so many ambiguities that the decree can be drawn to one shore or the other according as one adheres to the letter or lets oneself flow with the movement of the text in the dynamics and the undercurrents that have borne its genesis. This has been said, in particular, in order to invite us to vigilance. So many ventures, which are more and more numerous today and sometimes come from very high up, are now putting on Tridentine glasses to do their reading of Vatican II. This is a strange way to go beyond the texts, for it claims to advance the church by inviting it to draw back.

2. The evolution of Vatican II is just as remarkable in what concerns the christological foundations of the laity, or, more precisely, of the *baptismal priesthood*, that fundamental Christian notion to which one must unceasingly return in order to go beyond the very problem of the "laity."

The commentators on Vatican II have said again and again that the council refused to consider the priests and the bishops as an ecclesiastically isolated reality, that, on the contrary, it wanted to understand them in an explicit way *in* the mystery of a church that has been restored to all and thus does not belong to the clerics. The very construction of *Lumen Gentium* clearly manifests this intention. For its part, *The Ministry and Life of Priests* takes the time and trouble to begin the short section dedicated to "The Priesthood in the Mission of the Church" (no. 2) with a paragraph on the baptismal priesthood. It is surprising and remarkable that the christological foundations that are given there to the baptismal priesthood are precisely those that were used previously to justify the power of priests. It is indeed the eternal Christ, in effect, who radically justifies the baptismal priesthood, that which is common

(JESUS) CHRIST

to all Christians. This priesthood is resolved into a participation of the "whole mystical body . . . in the anointing by the Spirit with which he himself has been anointed." The word "anointed" is only the translation of the Greek word *Christos*, "Christ," and of the Hebrew word *Masiah*, "Messiah." For Jesus Christ, it is no longer "one title among others. It has become his proper name (when employed without the article) which sums up all the others. And those whom he has saved rightly bear the name 'Christian.' "[10] This at least means that believers are not baptized into only one pole of the mystery of Jesus Christ but into the totality of his personal mystery. No one has humanity and history as an exclusive possession, as his or her specific element, just as no one can appropriate for himself or herself the Christ of glory. Since everyone participates in the anointing of Easter, everyone receives God *and* the world, salvation *and* history, as an inheritance. It is against the background of this common dignity and of this common responsibility that the sacrament of the ordained ministry will perhaps be able to be understood.

The specific nature of the laity unfortunately continues to be defined by the *incarnation* of salvation in the world.[11] Who does not see the terrible danger? By returning the world and history to lay people, they are defined by that which even today is particularly perceived as escaping from the meaning of salvation. Structurally, lay people thus remain occupied with what is insane from a Christian and ecclesiastical point of view, whereas the clergy have a clear field for appropriating to themselves the Christ of glory and his work of mediation. But what disrespect for Vatican II! The latter does not justify the priesthood of all by the incarnation of salvation in a world that has no meaning of salvation. It is into the dead and resurrected Christ that all are baptized. It is the *totality* of the paschal mystery that thus answers for their priesthood. Let us immediately assess how *The Ministry and Life of Priests* thus offers us a vision all the more liberating than those to which we are accustomed.

73

3. Jesus Christ and the Future of the Laity

One thing is clear: lay men and women will be kept in passivity and submission as long as we have not experienced and reflected on the unique mediation of Jesus Christ in a different way. This is an immense task, let us repeat, since this mediation solicits the undivided attention of every christological reflection. Nevertheless, and in spite of evident limits, the refusal of every dichotomy proposes, in short, imperatives that everyone interested in the ecclesiastical future of the laity must make his or her own. Four paths are opened up which, through the mediation of Jesus Christ, specify the *Christian* meaning of God and thus express why (in virtue of what) it is necessary to change the present organization, an organization that only creates lay people because it has first created clerics.

Baptized into Easter

"To name God" and to see what our spontaneous images become when it is to the God of the *Christian* confession that one is referring was the first challenge noted in the preceding chapter. The confession of Jesus Christ as mediator prohibits all talk that situates God elsewhere than in the blank space that slips into the name itself of our savior. Such a meeting is little reassuring and somewhat disquieting, for, we said, nothing guarantees a priori that this space is not empty. Nevertheless, does that not suffice to refer us to the heart of the good news? Is a chance not offered to Christian persons and communities today that they might find the originality of the kerygma that the texts of the New Testament proclaim with such insistence? Jürgen Moltmann hears a similar invitation: "After the immovable, unfeeling countenance of the God of Plato, to which a few features of Stoic ethics were added, had looked upon theologians for such a long time from out of the image of Christ, the time for differentiating in view of the Christian faith the Father of Jesus Christ from the God of the pagans

(JESUS) CHRIST

and of the philosophers (Pascal) has finally come. That corresponds on the theoretical level to the critical disestablishment of Christianity with respect to the civil religions of their respective societies in which that theism prevails."[12] How is this "disestablishment" to be effected? It is into the Passover of Jesus Christ that all are baptized, and their God can only be a *God of the passage.* Jesus Christ thus does not establish us in the passive satisfaction of upstarts, in the static comfort of one world *or* the other, of the God of pure transcendence *or* of limits which, being absolutized, end by blocking history and killing it as history. Our God is the God of the passage itself. He thus devotes himself to living *in the act itself in which a human freedom is liberating itself.* The Christian faith thus refuses to measure the human weight of a person or of a collectivity according to the norms of whatever ideal, and especially one that would make use of God to sanction the absoluteness of its norms. The confession of Easter entails rather this other confession: every person and every collectivity is truly free that is somewhere beginning to *pass* elsewhere on the road of a promised and realized freedom.

But in order to be experienced and perceived as an encounter with God himself, passages require a conversion of the common ways of thinking and expressing Jesus Christ. He is not passively established in God, no more than he is entirely engulfed in the limits of his own history. He is *the way.* In the journey of our lives, he does not get lost in either the point of departure (the present situation of our personal and collective histories) or the imaginary point of arrival (God as he could be finally possessed). It is neither death only nor life only, but rather the *passage* that has become radically possible in him, and it is in this that he is eternally our mediator. The resurrection glorifies him as *wayfarer,* and that is what he is eternally, always making life arise from the very heart of death. It is in such a sense that we confess him as Lord. He is the eternal *ferryman* whose love never wearies of offering to humanity the possibility of constructing a *history of*

75

A CHURCH OF THE BAPTIZED

salvation and of freedom instead of being condemned to pursue the long story of egoism and betrayals of love.

Baptized into the passage, learning to seek Jesus Christ in the human passages that history offers to their lives, how could lay people passively abandon themselves into the hands of clerics? Clericalism is possible for two reasons: because clerics see themselves and are seen as men of God (or of the Christ of glory), and because, thanks to the passivity in which they maintain lay people, that would justify them in claiming to be the *agents of passage*. If this is how the "priesthood" of priests and bishops understands itself and is understood, it is simply not Christian. The confession of Easter restores to each Christian person and community the possibility and the responsibility of effecting their own passages. Who else could do so in their place if it is the case that history makes these passages to be their own? Thus, both clerics die *as* clerics and lay people die as lay people since the mediation of Jesus Christ is concretely denied as soon as *the relation itself* arises that creates a clergy and a laity.

Laity and Life in the Spirit
In virtue of what can all *effect a passage* and live their human history as the handwriting of salvation? They have themselves become mediators of salvation thanks to *baptism* which makes them "share in the anointing by the Spirit with which he himself has been anointed" and confers a "holy and royal priesthood" on them, to use the terms of Vatican II. These expressions may appear empty and without human content. They nevertheless reflect the heart of the Christian confession, the fundamental adherence without which nothing further would be possible. They confess nothing less than this: the Spirit is always faithfully offered through the gift of him whom he eternally anoints and eternally institutes as mediator between God and men. As a consequence, one can affirm that the baptismal condition consti-

tutes *an unsurpassable horizon of life, of intelligibility, and of action*. Nothing, absolutely nothing, can be experienced, understood, or done that can be situated *above* or *beside* the baptismal priesthood. In principle (in its principle which is the Spirit of Jesus Christ), the baptismal priesthood expresses the measure of Christian dignity and responsibility, a measure that is, properly speaking, without measure. Only the constant rediscovery of the baptismal priesthood as life in the Spirit can free Christian pride. This is a freeing without which, be it said in passing, there will continue to be many rebels and very few revolutionaries in the church.

In effect, when placed in relation to our christological heritage, this fundamental confession becomes foundational for entirely new relationships. Christian anthropology, which depends on christology in this matter, has essentially been an anthropology *of a lack*. Life and reflection continue to suffer cruelly from it. The dichotomies effected in the mystery of Jesus Christ nourished (and were nourished by) a conception of history that, in the best of cases, has the latter walk on a road parallel to the ways of salvation and, in the worst, erects history as the opposite of salvation. The historical condition of Christian existence thus condemns it to a "lack," an exhausting pursuit of a salvation that unceasingly continues to escape from it. The baptismal priesthood affirms, on the contrary, a salvation that is always coming *because it is always there*, a salvation offered in all grace, a prevenient gratuitousness, which unceasingly offers the possibility of reopening history.

Since nothing can be situated outside, beside, or above the baptismal priesthood, Christian individuals and communities thus find in baptism all that is necessary in order radically to refuse every form of clericalism, including certain views of what is called the "priesthood" of priests and bishops, views whose concrete result is to institute priests and bishops in a "super-Christian" state.

A CHURCH OF THE BAPTIZED

As an Excess

One does not deny the unique mediation of Jesus Christ from the sole fact that one rejects certain disastrous ways of thinking of it as a unidirectional movement going *from* the divinity *to* the humanity. Positively speaking, this rejection invites one rather to encounter the following demand: in order that Jesus Christ may truly mediate salvation, his humanity (including his death) must enter in a defining element of the mystery of Easter. Without this there is quite simply no Easter, no passage, since the very thing that is to effect a passage to God is absent from the passage. But this assumption of the humanity of Jesus into the paschal mystery is itself possible only in virtue of another encounter that founds it: what has been glorified at the resurrection is nothing other than the history of *this* man Jesus, his human ways of discovering and living his relation to others and to God, his incessant quest for human and historical freedom, with all that this quest implies of discovery but also of struggles, hesitation, suffering, and doubt. As a result, our theistic visions are called to conversion: "As a theology of the cross, Christian theology is the critique and liberation of philosophical and political monotheism. Theism says that God cannot suffer, God cannot die, in order to take the suffering, mortal being under his protection. Christian faith says that God suffered in the suffering of Jesus, God died on the cross of Christ, in order that we might live and rise in his future."[13] In order for the Christian experience to be possible, however, it is necessary to see that the resurrection calls of itself for the other pole, that of the human history of Jesus. Without this, the mediation is rendered impossible, and it is really absurd to confess Jesus Christ as the unique mediator between God and man. What the Spirit glorifies eternally at the resurrection is thus the human meaning that Jesus gave to his history and nothing else.

That is the mediator whom Christians invoke, and that is

(JESUS) CHRIST

why *their baptismal priesthood has no other place to exist and to be expressed than history and its limits.* It will still be said that their world (all that awaits a definitive liberation in a given place of their space and a given moment of their history) is the *condition of possibility* of a salvation that is truly Christian. All the dimensions of human existence thus enter into the historical work of God, from the most long-term to the most short-term relations, from personal and interpersonal relations to those that weave the tissue of the political universe and those that place all the people of the earth in economic intercommunication. There is no true passage, no truly Christian passage, if all these things are not effecting a passage. The confession of the Christian priesthood affirms a saved freedom that only exists when it is working effectively for a liberation of history. That is how the Christian faith can convert all humanly reductive religious anthropologies and all relationships to the sacred that alienate personal and collective freedoms.

By definition, the clergy is defined *only* by the top. Should one be amazed by the fact that it has become humanly insignificant? This human insignificance points, in any case, to another lack that is properly of the nature of the Christian faith: the loss of human meaning itself depends on the fact that the idea of a clergy is insane from a Christian point of view. This is what is lived and said as soon as believing persons and communities actualize the encounter with God and with historical limits *in* a work of historical liberation. The way of life of clerics, their actions and their speech, appear literally ex-centric in relation to the human places where the fate of salvation and that of human history are simultaneously being decided. As soon as lay people discover that their historical freedom is the place of salvation, they also learn that the clergy, as defined by their relations with it, is a reality unworthy of God, absurd, unjustifiable, and thus unacceptable from a Christian point of view.

Deciding

Is it possible to go beyond the preceding considerations? Can one go beyond the statement, according to which God and history are definitively reconciled in Jesus Christ the mediator, and tell the *place* of this reconciliation with greater precision? To take up again the terminology employed above, does Jesus Christ, the eternal ferryman, effect a passage in our place, thus favoring our abdication?

The passivity of Jesus came from the fact that his human freedom was, in relation to his saving act, only a powerless toy at the mercy of the divinity. Losing it either entirely in God or entirely in the events of his historical existence, believers situated this act everywhere but where his mediation can be understood otherwise than as an absurd dichotomization of his person: *in the human decision in favor of God.* Baptized into him, we participate in this decision in the Spirit. One thus understands the correctness of this statement of François Varillon: "It is important that Christ be situated *where he is*, i.e., *in our freedom to act*, i.e., *in our decisions.*"[14] Christians are constantly led to seek Jesus Christ "in the heavens" or in a "world" where they would no longer have *humanly to decide* in favor of salvation. Their only way of resisting the attraction of this double flight is constantly to restore the mediation of Jesus Christ to their own historical decisions, to their acts of freedom which involve both God and the world. That is the place where the fate of salvation *and* of history is decided; that is where it is given to them to mediate the unique action of the mediator.

Such a shift inevitably involves a conversion of relationships with God as the baptized have learned to understand them. Rather than sanction absolutely the passivity of human beings, the God of Jesus Christ so restores freedom to itself that human beings have become responsible to him for their fate and their existence in history. Before the convulsions of history, one often asks about the presence or absence of God. The answer will

(JESUS) CHRIST

always escape from minds that place it elsewhere than in human history. In the person of the mediator, François Varillon writes, "God creates creators."[15] And the stature of these creators, the scope of their responsibility, is measured by the fact that they have to decide even about the historical existence of God. However little it should be and can be understood in such a sense, the mediation of Jesus Christ forbids historical relations where the ones would "possess" God and be able to transmit him, whereas the others would be an empty receptacle capable at the most of receiving.

Concerning our question, this means that the personal mystery of Jesus Christ condemns the relation itself that makes there to be "clerics" and "lay people" in the church. All who have been baptized in the unique mediator, all Christians, have become *the subject of salvation*. As the sacrament of such a salvation, the church must thus structure itself in a manner that permits all effectively, i.e., "in fact," to be *the subject of ecclesiastical life*.

4

Priests

"The Priest Is Another Christ"

Through Christ, God gives to *priests* a power over the mass. In the religious landscape of believers, the priests constitute the third link of the chain. Does God intervene directly to elevate priests to the status of *active subject?* And, if so, how are priests then invited to situate themselves with respect to the bottom, or, more particularly, in their relations to lay people? These are two questions that tell the extent to which our reflection now approaches in a more direct way the theological justification that has been given to the present structure of clergy/laity relationships.

Our heritage told us that the celebration of the mass constituted the end of the "priesthood" of priests, and the Council of Trent greatly contributed to attributing this end to them as their proper domain. This tells us sufficiently why the bishops and the pope are not explicitly in question, for, as the result of Trent, there is "a certain confusion that has weighed quite heavily on later theology. In effect, to seek the meaning of the institution of the presbyterate solely from the power of celebrating the eucharist is, in a certain way, to condemn oneself to putting the apostles, the bishops, and the priests on the same level. . . . All the members of the hierarchy have the same 'priesthood,' understood in a univocal fashion, in common."[1] From this perspective, one is speaking of one and the same reality, because of the univocity of understanding, when one treats of the priests, the bishops, or the pope.

But before asking about the eucharist (which will be the subject of the next chapter), and thus before reflecting on the specific end of the priesthood of priests, a task imposes itself: to see how, in the schema, the *direction of the arrows* itself determines the place of the priests in the ecclesiological logic and the ecclesiastical structure. Too many present ventures are devoted only to "broadening" the end of the presbyterate. They neglect, however, the prior moment, a capital one for me, of a reflection on the *relation* itself that situates the place of the priests in the church. One notices more and more the harmful results of this negligence: clericalism changes ends; it is no longer defined solely by a power over the mass, but it remains fundamentally what it is, i.e., a management of ecclesiastical relationships in which everything goes only from the top to the bottom. Hence an ambiguity that has lasted since Vatican II: through lack of an effective conversion of the ecclesiological logic and of the ecclesiastical structure, the priests, the bishops, and the pope may well utilize a vocabulary of *service* at the same time they continue to have behavior patterns of *power*.

The preceding chapter directly demands rather that one first reflect on *the type of mediation* employed in thinking about the priesthood of priests. In my opinion, such is the immediate ideological foundation of clerical power that has condemned lay persons to passivity.

1. Priestly Mediation

The preceding chapter concluded that an exclusively deductive logic cannot account for the mediation of Jesus Christ in a way valid from the Christian point of view. Nevertheless, if salvation is *for us*, it must reach us in the moment that is ours, in the corner of the earth that we inhabit. Since the mediation of Jesus Christ has been understood according to a logic that frustrates it for all practical purposes, our heritage was obliged to set up *other* mediators, and it is indeed in this way that the priests came to be situated in the

83

A CHURCH OF THE BAPTIZED

dynamics of Christian and ecclesiastical life. "In a general sense, a mediator is one who or that which, in one way or another, establishes or supports between two others a relation that would not or could not exist without him or it."[2] To put it briefly, priests and bishops are thus seen as the *mediators of the mediation of Jesus Christ*. But does this mediation of the priest as "another Christ" succeed more than of Jesus Christ himself?

The Situation of Priests in the Church

Let us first listen to the vocabulary, for it is never theologically innocent. Yves Congar, no doubt one of our best specialists in the history of ecclesiologies and a pioneer in what concerns the theology of the laity, finds in the past the following expressions (which, of course, he does not take up as his own): "The priest is *superior* to the angels and similar to Mary, since his role is to *give* Jesus, to *make him come*; he is even *more powerful* than Mary, since she *gave birth* to Jesus *only once*, whereas he can make him come *a thousand times*."[3] Today such formulae spontaneously make one smile. They are nevertheless only the crystallized expression, so to speak, of a logic that once structured mentalities. Are we free from this logic by the sole fact that our language has been purified of its most evident excesses? From this point of view, the italicized words in the citation underline *three aims* of our most immediate heritage, three intentions important for the priests themselves, but which were equally proposed to all Christians. They have accustomed lay persons to not situating themselves in any way in their relationships with the clergy.

1. The vocabulary first vigorously affirms the *power* of the priest. All the expressions chosen take this direction: the power of the priest is superior to that of the angels; it surpasses even that of Mary. One guesses that these strong statements are not without consequence for the way of determining the place of priests in ecclesiastical life and organization, that they let the presbyterate slide to the side of an historical *power*.

84

2. In virtue of their power and in order that it be respected, priests must *elevate themselves* or *be elevated* as high as possible. If they are above even the angels and Mary, where will they stand in their relations to lay people? The place reserved for them in the schema is thus illustrated: they enter in immediately after God and Christ.

3. Finally, it is necessary to underline a third characteristic, one essential for understanding the global character of the landscape within which life and reflection have understood the priesthood of the priests: one is functioning here within an extremely *objectifying* and *reifying* universe. The words themselves express this; they speak of *giving* Jesus, of *making him come*, and do not fear "quantifying" this coming (Mary has given Jesus only *once*, whereas the priest can do it *a thousand times*).

Mediators between God and Men

One better understands now why the priest perceives himself and has been perceived as *"another Christ."* In order to specify his status further, would it not be necessary to say that, in the schema and with respect to the church of history, he situates himself *immediately* after God? Thanks to their power over the mass, the priests control, in effect, the coming of Jesus into history. Hence a question before which reflection cannot shy away: Do not our spontaneous visions place the priest even above Jesus Christ? This is something that merits an attentive analysis and suggests the magnitude of the challenges that face life and reflection today. The image of the priest as "another Christ" bears a long history; it has left a deep mark on people's mentalities. The church will thus not be freed from it tomorrow or the day after tomorrow.[4] This image reflects a certain understanding of the *mediation* of priests and can only be corrected if the logic itself according to which this mediation is experienced and thought is corrected.

In a thousand ways, in effect, the common vocabulary still says that the priest is *mediator between God and men*. But the terms

A CHURCH OF THE BAPTIZED

qualify this mediation: the "between" points to the fact that one continues to think of the priest as a mediator of the *physical causality* type. This "other Christ" exists and acts in the manner of a pipe that, being situated between the reservoir and the faucet, permits the water to pass from the reservoir to the faucet. As a link that joins God and men, it is still said that the priest is a bridge between God and them (hence the expression, pregnant with meaning, that still describes the pope: pontiff, *pontifex*, builder of bridges). In his relationship with the laity, the priest is the bridge that assures the passage from one shore to the other. He permits lay people to pass over to the side of God and the latter to enter into their lives. Let us anticipate the next chapter: it is at the mass that the priest finds the eminent expression of his being and his mission since he there exercises his power of consecrating, of *making* the body and blood of Christ *pass* into the bread and wine; thanks to him, lay people have the possibility of "receiving" communion.

Among all the activities of the priest, that which he accomplishes at mass is thus the most noble. But one must not cover up the fact that the situation of the priest at mass is only the privileged expression of the place that clerics occupy in the *entire* organization of the church. That is why, above and beyond the particular end entrusted to the mediation of the priests, it is necessary to go back to the *logic* of the mediation and to analyze the dynamics that it sets in motion. Since Vatican II, the priests and bishops who will define themselves by a "power of saying the mass" are, in fact, rare. Nevertheless, does saying that priests and bishops have the mission of "creating" the unity of the church, as I often hear, not take up the same dynamics? They are the mediators of something else, but they understand themselves according to the same type of mediation.

It is necessary to underline two fundamental privileges that this type of mediation confers on the clergy. Whether they have the power of saying the mass, of creating unity, or of something else, clerics have control of the process of *production*. We have

86

seen this with regard to the production of the "official" moral discourse of the church. This first privilege already comprises grave implications: a priori, the clergy know what lay persons must do (or produce) in order to be in the truth of the church. Furthermore, priests and bishops control the *finished product*: they can verify a posteriori if a given practice, attitude, or behavior is truly "of the church." Structurally, the priests, the bishops, and the pope thus *thoroughly* control the content of ecclesiastical life. As I said above, they simultaneously hold the legislative power, the executive power, and the judicial power. That is how the mediation of which they are in charge imposes them in fact as *the* subject of the life of the church.

The Crisis of the Priesthood

"Who are we, the priests of Quebec? We are the object of numerous conversations, questions, and surveys. We question ourselves regularly about our *identity*, our integration into the church of today, *without ever obtaining any definitive answer.*"[5] Everything indicates that the clergy (of Quebec and elsewhere!) have not yet emerged from an identity crisis that has deeply shaken it, especially in the last few decades.

Innumerable studies have appeared on what is called "the priestly malaise." Psychological, sociological, even political approaches—all disciplines have been turned to good account. Without denying their inestimable contribution, one can ask oneself: if the malaise is so deep and so lasting, is it not that the very foundations of the theology of the presbyterate have been challenged, the logic that was brought into play to establish the "power" of the clerics and to determine their place in the church? Today one comes to this finding which, at first glance, is surprising: lay persons have been able to feel (and still feel) excluded from the life and the organization of the church as much as priests and bishops experience a profound crisis of ecclesiastical identity.[6]

A CHURCH OF THE BAPTIZED

Before being taken up by reflection, this crisis, like all crises, is provoked by questions that arise from life. The priests, the bishops, and the pope understand themselves and are understood as responsible for a passage to be effected; they thus see themselves and are seen after the fashion of a *third term* between the two poles that they have the mission of reconciling. But, in doing so, "one has limited oneself to introducing a third term that is itself *exterior to the first two*."[7] And that is, in my opinion, the first reason for the malaise of the clerics. On the one hand, they are asked to give God to people. But once in contact with a laity that is deeply involved in the world in the name of its faith (just think of the members of Catholic Action), they become aware that they are not "objectively" closer to God, that they do not possess God any more than those to whom they are supposed to give God. In a world undergoing profound change, on the other hand, they are progressively realizing to what extent they can be detached from the other pole and be "exterior" to the world and to those who have received this world as their proper domain, the lay people. The strangeness of their discourse already manifests to what extent the world is far from them and that they have a very weak hold on it. In other words, as a bridge built between two shores, the clergy doubts more and more its real foundations on both shores. It is in this way that the christological question encountered in the preceding chapter is inevitably raised: At bottom, are the pope, the bishops, and the priests not asked to succeed where Christ has failed? Such does indeed seem to be the question that life has posed and still poses for the reflection of believing persons and communities.

A Mediation That Mediates Nothing

The being and the mission that had devolved upon priests reposes on christological foundations that the Christian faith is learning to judge as intolerable. A dichotomy is, in effect, presupposed which, even after the death and resurrection of Jesus Christ, locks God and the world into two solitudes which cannot communicate without the clerics. A *gap* persists that necessitates the intervention of the clergy and its mediation. But does not the mission thus entrusted to the priest directly undermine the *unicity* of the priesthood and the mediation of Jesus Christ?[8] From a Christian point of view, a reified mediation cannot explain the place of the pope, the bishops, and the priests in the life of the church. One can well see, in effect, that "to seek mediation on this path is to be referred to an indefinite series of intermediary terms that would, however, be unable to fill the abyss *that has first been dug*. If Jesus is a mediator in this sense, i.e., if while positing Jesus Christ one maintains the *exteriority* between God and humanity, it is then necessary, in effect, to have intervene a mediation by the Virgin, Saint Joseph, the sacraments, the hierarchy, etc., *without ever exiting from exteriority*."[9]

A problem that we have already sketched out previously is thus made more critical. As a bridge built between God and the world, an intermediate term that has slipped between two other terms, the clergy prevents the Christian people from seeing that in Jesus Christ the mediator *everything* has already been perfectly reconciled.

A *Contemporary Theology*

Does Christian thought today give sufficient attention to the type of mediation that is operative in determining the place of priests and bishops in the economy of ecclesiastical life? One may entertain some doubt. In order to flesh out this question, I am going to question the theology that Pierre Grelot proposes in his "critical dialogue with Edward Schillebeeckx."[10] We shall see that, even if his theology dons new vestments, it makes use of the type of reified mediation of which I have just spoken.

Grelot's study unfolds in the field of exegesis and, from this point of view, addresses the specialists of this discipline first of all. Nevertheless, as we shall see, it cannot help making use of a

A CHURCH OF THE BAPTIZED

certain theology and is therefore of interest to all theologians, whatever the respective specialization of their disciplines. At this particular moment of the argument, the question that our reflection addresses to Grelot is thus the following: *What type of mediation* does this theology bring into play when it speaks of priests and bishops?

Grelot essentially relies on the statement according to which "the apostolic tradition has handed down to the church of all centuries *normative structures* outside of which it is illusory to speak of 'ecclesiastical communities.' "[11] All valid reflection on these normative structures must therefore take account of "the action of the apostles, the direct envoys of the Christ of glory."[12] This is where the ministry of priests and bishops lies. Every minister is, in effect, "sent in the wake of the apostles and in their succession in order to render sensible the effective presence of the risen one who opens his table to the members of his church."[13]

The presence of the risen one, Grelot affirms, passes to the church "by a solid and verifiable chain of 'succession' ":[14] *"The ecclesiastical relation to the risen Christ and the presiding at his meal are passed on by the mediation of his direct envoys, the apostles.* They are then passed on by those who cooperate with their action in order to extend its effects unto the extremities of the world by announcing the gospel that has been entrusted to them and by exercising the responsibilities that they have, not from the communities, but from the founders, who are themselves linked to the apostles of Christ."[15]

But the decisive question which Grelot never confronts explicitly bears on this "passing on" by the ministers of the life of the risen Christ. What type of mediation do they exercise there thanks to their ties with the apostles? What sort of "ferrymen" are they? Everything leads one to believe that Grelot's theology functions within the schemas of physical causality.

One can spatialize the third term that has been in question, consider it as a pipe that, while placing the reservoir and the

90

PRIESTS

faucet in relation, keeps its proper space. Because we have bodies, and because human freedom cannot understand itself without dispersing itself in space, such is probably the image that most spontaneously arises when one reflects on reified mediation. But the relationship with time can also be organized according to the same logic. The third term is then introduced between a past moment and the present moment in order to make the first pass into the second thanks to an objectification of relationships that is the same as in spatial mediation.

Does Grelot's theology function in this way? It seems to form an objectifying and reifying conception of time and history. A first indication of this is that, according to him, the ministers "prolong the initial mission of the apostles through the centuries."[16] Is this prolongation to be understood according to the schemas of physical causality? The term "prolongation" itself leads one to believe so. This is why W. Kaspar, for his part, rejects this term: "The priesthood of Christ thus has no need of being *prolonged* nor of being *completed* by other human priests. His priesthood is the consummation of every priesthood; with him, every priesthood has reached its end."[17] Furthermore, this first impression is confirmed when Grelot renders explicit the tie between the sub-apostolic period and the following period. The vocabulary employed (especially the term "channel," which refers directly to the order of things) and the logical ordering of historical moments present history as a smooth, unbroken "continuity" (according to his own expression). In effect, if there is "continuity" between the sub-apostolic period and the following, it is through the "continuity" of a "communal praxis" that *"thus constitutes a channel of transmission which one must carefully take into account. It is a less immediate channel than the New Testament itself, but still an important one. . . ."*[18]

The true nature of this ministerial mediation appears still more clearly when one measures the disastrous consequences to which Grelot's theology leads. The latter says, in effect, that "the

91

A CHURCH OF THE BAPTIZED

holders of the apostolic succession, outside of which there is no
church, are in fact responsible for the lives of groups of Christians
who desire to be linked in a concrete fashion to the church."[19] He
even specifies that the minister "has received *the responsibility* for
ecclesiastical life."[20] In virtue of what can priests and bishops
appropriate to themselves "the" responsibility for the church?
Have the non-ministers not just been condemned to passivity and
to ecclesiastical inertia? And what permits one to withdraw the
"apostolic succession" from the churches themselves (lay people
included) in order to give it to the bishops and priests as their
exclusive possession? Grelot does not seem to take much away
from lay people when he entrusts this succession to the ministers.
But even if it is exercised in the narrowest possible field, physical
mediation always ends in the same result. In the end, it always
makes the *entire* ecclesiastical responsibility flow from the top,
i.e., from the priests and the bishops. It thus concretely forbids
the affirmation according to which all believing persons and
communities are the *subject* of their life in the church.

2. "Simple Lay People"

Even in contemporary theology, it seems that the schemes
of physical causality continue their ravages. In one way or another, the clergy thus continues to be perceived as having the
power of giving the life of Jesus Christ to lay people. The latter
constitute the term of the passage to which the privilege of "receiving" the things of salvation is given and no other. It is in this very
thing that the clergy *institutes* the laity as a reality *defined by the
negative.* "The priest is the one who has received the power (it
being understood that lay people *have not*) of celebrating the
eucharist and of forgiving sins."[21] Even if one broadens the end of
the power, the eucharist being judged too restrictive, an identical
relationship is maintained: one pole gives and transmits, whereas
something is given and transmitted to the other.

92

Furthermore, what vocabulary is employed to express this second pole of the binomial? In our day, one still speaks spontaneously of "simple lay people," of "simple baptized people," or of the "simple faithful," letting it be understood thereby that the priests are as "superior" as lay people are in an ecclesiastical position of inferiority. Many commentators have noted the fact that Vatican II has reversed the pyramidal organization constructed by this distribution of *more* and *less*. It has been rightly said that the council has restored the church to all believers and to all believing communities. One could think that, in accord with this program, lay persons would have hastened to become the subject of the church. Is this indeed the case? In spite of the numerous initiatives that tend in this direction, the vast majority delays in taking charge of this church that one wished to return to all.

There is no need of a long demonstration to support this general judgment. Let one simply ask: *Who* is the church? The test is even more revealing when one merely listens attentively to the spontaneous ways in which people continue to express the church. One discovers, in effect, that it is practically always identified with a particular person (the pope), a collective person (the bishops, the priests), or a moment of space (the parish and the diocese) or of time (the Sunday mass). There is no question here of denying all ecclesiastical status to the pope, the clergy, the parish, or the Sunday mass. What it is necessary to underline, and what is deeply revealing, however, is that the church is still *identified* with persons, places, or moments that remain *external* to the Christian experience of lay people. But how can one be the subject of a reality that one continues to situate *outside* oneself?

The important question is "Why?" Why, globally speaking, do Christians still have the tendency to transfer the church outside their existences, to the exterior of their lives? Why do they delay in becoming the subject of the church? The answer is evident: for a long time they have learned to leave the church in

A CHURCH OF THE BAPTIZED

the hands of clerics. But the refusal to see the priests as a reified mediation permits one to support this answer while singling out more clearly the reasons for the passivity of lay people. The logic of reified mediation can, in effect, only work in virtue of *a triple dichotomy*. And the exploration of these three caesurae constitutes an imperative for whoever desires to give the laity its entire ecclesiastical chance again.

The Clergy/Laity Separation

On the most immediate level, a separation between clerics and lay people is being experienced. The church and church responsibilities belong to the first group, whereas lay people, ecclesiastically speaking, have nothing and are nothing.

Certainly, lay people are being invited more and more to *participate* in the life of the church. Shortly after the last council, the clergy set up numerous structures of participation. To take only one example, pastoral councils, both parochial and diocesan, have arisen almost everywhere, and numerous lay people have become involved and expend great energies on them. But one is entitled to ask: Does participation in these councils as well as in other bodies suffice to effect the change of subject that Vatican II desired? The language that is spoken there remains to a great extent a language of *adaptation* of the existing ecclesiastical structures, the participation having for its essential end to help the parishes and the dioceses to "adapt" to the changes of our times. One looks for livelier and more attractive liturgies, the organization of more adequate charitable services, even the institution here and there of structured groups who will be particularly concerned about those who are distant, etc.

It is to be hoped that this participation will progressively serve truly to provoke the conversion that one is entitled to expect as soon as one believes that all believing persons and communities are the subject of the church. But it is necessary to recognize the insufficiency of the structural initiatives that have

94

been taken. Has the old logic exploded? Simple lay people have joined pastoral councils but in order that the parish or diocesan structures, remaining fundamentally identical to what they were, *may go toward* Christians or non-Christians in a more effective manner. The dynamic being served is the same: *from* the parish or *from* the diocese *toward* the world and history. There is really no challenging of the ecclesiastical structures as they articulate their relationships with the world, with the bottom. Hence the ecclesiastically unacceptable situation in which so many lay people find themselves today: either they are not involved because, according to them, the ecclesiastical structures have ceased to have historical relevance, or they participate but in the constant fear of being taken over by the existing structures and of being clericalized themselves. Both cases, each in its own way, reveal the same dichotomy, a first level that separates clerics and lay people.

A Divorce Between Faith and Church

The first separation is only the visible part of the iceberg. It depends on the understanding that is had of the priest-mediator and, as such, indicates a deeper and more devastating dichotomy.

Christians today are experiencing difficulties in establishing a tie between the *church* and their *faith*. Insofar as the place of priests has been experienced and reflected on as a physical and reified mediation, it is in the priests and bishops that the ecclesiastical meaning of the Christian life has come to be exhausted. They are the church. As I have often said, this identification of the church with the members of the clergy is even more manifest everywhere today.[22] Nevertheless, the harmful results of this seizure have hardly begun to be measured. In particular, it is easy to see to what extent lay people have not learned to seek the church *in* their act of faith itself, in the most *personal* aspect of this act of faith, where they could perhaps discover that every act of faith is communal by nature.[23] Are there many lay people today who

95

A CHURCH OF THE BAPTIZED

spontaneously say: *"I am church"*? And, above all, do they live accordingly?

The divorce between faith and church brings about strange phenomena. For example, at the same time that numerous traditionally Christian countries are experiencing a vertiginous drop in what is called the "practice of religion," the great majority of people continue to call themselves believers. But where does the ecclesiastical meaning of this faith reside? Does it have only one? The extreme form of the paradox is that, having rediscovered the communal dimension of the Christian faith and in the name of this discovery, some have distanced themselves from the church because the latter, they say, is presently an obstacle to a truly communal life. Furthermore, there are many who continue to refer to Jesus. In certain places, he is even experiencing a gain in popularity. The surprising thing is that the ecclesiastical consequences of this new popularity are not being seen.

It is not exaggerated to say that lay people have for a long time learned to live their faith as "something between God (or Jesus) and me." The clergy/laity separation is thus revelatory of a more fundamental divorce that has broken the ties between faith and the church. Faith concerns "vertical" relations; but it is still difficult to see that it necessarily entails a new type of "horizontal" relations also where the church would find its natural habitat, so to speak.

When Christians find the ties between faith and the church again, when they rediscover that the church is part of even the most personal act of faith, the present state of ecclesiastical organization experiences inevitable convulsions. Numerous experiences here and there already express the type of questions that then come to be posed for the consciousness of the believer. What is to become of parishes and dioceses, for example, if Christians who take the statement seriously that they are the subject of the church equally understand that they are the subject of it *in everything* that constitutes them as believing human persons? Can they continue to believe that an "I," even a believing one, can live humanly true ecclesiastical relations when the *only* recognized place of ecclesiastical life offers the meeting of two hundred or five hundred other "I's"? In short, the parish and the diocese are today the only mode of ecclesiastical life (for the vast majority of lay people and in the mind of many clerics), which will either explode or be obliged to define themselves differently.

The Faith/History Dichotomy

Once the first two levels have been crossed, an invitation is issued to explore a third. If the clergy and the laity have been so separated, if the relationships between faith and church have ceased to be seen, it is because a first caesura, without a doubt one foundational for the other two, has dichotomized the relationships between *faith* and *history*.

Have we truly learned that faith is part of our historical existence and that the latter is part of the former? More precisely, it is easily enough conceived that faith can have consequences for the way the history of our personal and collective lives is managed. But faith is then considered as a reservoir *from which* one draws the norms that guide (or are imposed on) our existence in history. Hence the question: Does what we are as historical beings, who inhabit the world but are also *inhabited* by it, affect faith or the dynamics of our lives of faith in one way or the other? The logic remains a descending one: faith exists "somewhere," as a pure nucleus, as a light that can illuminate our personal and collective histories without the reverse movement being possible.

But if history is an empty vase, capable at most of receiving "objects" of the faith, how does the Christian faith truly make us the subjects of our lives? Does it constitute an encounter at this immediate point with God, which it would claim is the same always and everywhere and which it would suffice to apply to the moment that we are living and to the corner of space that we

A CHURCH OF THE BAPTIZED

inhabit? The reified mediation of the clerics gives a clear answer to these questions: the bottom cannot define what is situated on top, and what is at stake historically has no hold on the faith.

3. Toward a Conversion of Clergy/Laity Relations

Vatican II invites us to a conversion of the ecclesiastical pyramid. It should now be clear that this conversion will remain a nice principle, a gratuitous invitation, that the texts can allow themselves without life being changed as long as the structure itself that presently organizes the relations between clerics and lay people is not turned upside down. [24]

The conversion is thus impossible unless the ecclesiastical status of those who continue to be called lay people is reevaluated. Should one conclude from that, as many lay people but above all clerics let it be understood, that this reevaluation is paid for by a sort of depreciation of the presbyterate and the episcopate? The movement does not respond to such grossly symmetrical beats, and this conclusion appears quite simplistic. I am personally convinced of the contrary. The only theological chance for the presbyterate and the episcopate is to rethink their tie with that unsurpassable reality which is the baptismal priesthood. That is the only way as well of liberating the existence of priests and bishops from a type of mediation that, because it is not justifiable from a Christian point of view in the first place, makes life really impossible for them. In effect, the rediscovery of the *unicity* of the priestly mediation of Jesus Christ "already constitutes (for priests), from a simple human point of view, a considerable relief. It liberates one from a complex of otherwise unbearable responsibilities. Since Jesus Christ is and remains the one and only priest, the human responsibility for the salvation of others in general first becomes bearable and even assumable as a result. It is bearable insofar as one believes that Jesus is the Lord to whom history and thus the future belong."[25]

98

I should, however, add that the presbyteral and episcopal service is not humanly viable unless, by rediscovering the unicity of the priesthood of Christ, one recognizes a single historical participation in this priesthood, that which constitutes precisely the *baptismal priesthood.* In order to liberate the ministers, the latter must first be respected as the Christian authority that permits the ecclesiastical status of the laity to be freed. It is thus in function of it that the present ecclesiastical structures must be rethought. *Four points* will indicate (too rapidly) the openness that life and reflection are invited to create.

Lay Persons Authorized To Mediate Salvation

The refusal of one form of mediation does not imply that *all* mediation is rejected. Reified mediation justifies the clerical church because it simultaneously sanctions both the active status of clerics (they are the *agents* of salvation and of ecclesiastical life) and the *passive* status of lay persons (they can only *receive* both salvation and the church). As I have said, the present status of the laity is ultimately an insult to the very mystery of Jesus Christ and to his mediation. It presupposes that this mediation functions as things function and that the humanity of Jesus is only the object of an arbitrary good will of God. But the priestly mediation of Jesus Christ must be situated *in* Easter itself, *in the passage.* It then becomes unacceptable to set up other mediators who, by arrogating to themselves a monopoly on the term into which all should pass (God and salvation), deprive persons and communities of the right and the responsibility of seeking salvation in the historical passages that they have been called to live. The christological foundations of an anthropology are thus singled out which bursts the alienating dreams of *immediacy* and for which *everything* in the Christian life can only be experienced and thought of *in the mode of mediation.*

The priesthood "of all the baptized consists in an ontological participation in that of Christ which constitutes precisely the

A CHURCH OF THE BAPTIZED

existence of the Christian life itself."[26] In speaking of the baptismal priesthood, does one refer to anything other than Christian and ecclesiastical *being?* At the very least, that means that the activity of Christ the mediator is not operative today thanks to the power of things or of persons who would be entirely *external* to believers and to communities, as clericalism would have it understood. The actuality of the mediation of Jesus Christ must be sought, on the contrary, *in the being* of all Christians, in the historical exercise of their believing freedom. Furthermore, if this mediation of Jesus Christ makes a gift of freedom (and thus of responsibility), how could lay persons still tolerate a type of relation to the clergy that endures solely in virtue of a rejection of their status as an active subject and thus by a negation of their Christian dignity and responsibility? More directly, do the presbyterate and the episcopate still have a *Christian* meaning when the "simple baptized" have been deprived of the responsibility of themselves *making them exist* as *one* particular sacrament in the economy of a church that has been restored to all? I believe that only the historical answer to this question will permit the Church to exit from the present contradiction. It alone will tell whether the change of ecclesiological perspectives is only a matter of high-flown principle, one that sounds nice in the texts and in the rhetoric of the discourses that try to rouse lay people to enthusiasm but one that changes nothing in the historical course of the ecclesiastical organization.

"A *Difference in Essence and Not Only in Degree*"

Lumen Gentium 10 clearly affirms that the baptismal priesthood, on the one hand, and the presbyterate and the episcopate, on the other, "differ from one another in essence and not only in degree." It is a surprising phenomenon that this text is often taken up in order to suggest that priests and bishops "are evidently not only lay people" and that they thus have something "more." In doing so, one only sets up degrees and denies the essential difference that is affirmed by Vatican II. How is this essential difference to be understood? It is precisely this difference that is going to define the relations that are possible from a Christian point of view between lay people and those (priests, bishops, and pope) in whom clericalism exhausts the action of the church.

Because it is of the nature of *Christian being*, and because it affirms the participation of all in the unique mediation of Jesus Christ, the preceding chapter concluded that the baptismal priesthood must be understood as *an unsurpassable horizon of life, intelligibility, and action.* The present moment of the argument allows us to specify that this horizon, which is definitive of the Christian life, forbids that any *other* mediator be able to interpose himself *between* Jesus Christ and believers. Since the introduction of this third term, in effect, it has just been affirmed that the baptismal priesthood is surpassable and has been surpassed, and it dies as an unsurpassable reality. One withdraws with one hand what was given with the other. On the one hand, the baptismal priesthood is confessed as the *fullness* of historical participation in the priesthood of Christ; on the other, life is lived (and organized) as if there could be another priesthood of the same order distinguishing itself only by "degree." It would be as well to say that the baptismal priesthood dies *as a fullness.* Unless faith condemns us to the absurdity of contradiction, *there cannot be in history any other Christian priesthood than the baptismal priesthood,* there can be no other priesthood that would number with it within a homogeneous whole.

To say and to live anything else is to contradict *Lumen Gentium:* these two priesthoods could only be thought of in terms of "more" and "less." The vision of the priest-mediator, such as recent centuries have handed it on to us, furthermore makes of the priest a *"super-Christian."*[27] As more a Christian than the "simple" Christians, this cleric resides above lay people and can thus arrogate to himself the monopoly on ecclesiastical life. But this seizure is possible only by a reduction of the baptized to the

A CHURCH OF THE BAPTIZED

state of lay people, of those who have nothing and do nothing, in the face of those who have all, can do all, and do do all.

Baptismal Priesthood and the Service of Ordained Ministers

Putting the church back into the hands of all believing persons and communities thus remains a pious wish if, during this time, one continues to force life into the old structures. This discourse is even dangerous, for it can put the Christian consciousness to sleep while, at the level of the functioning of the organization, certain ones bustle about to reinforce the old ways of being and acting. But life can become intolerable so quickly when there is not a minimum of consistency between what is said and what is done. Before the church becomes unlivable for an even greater number of Christians, the structures must be adjusted to what faith confesses. On the level of the life of the church, the confession of the baptismal priesthood is reflected in this other confession: since believers, thanks to baptism, are the subject of ecclesiastical life, all persons and communities are authorized by Jesus Christ during the time of history to be *the first and last guarantor of the church*. How much there is to say about this with respect to clergy/laity relations! But that would exceed the limited objective of this work. I shall content myself with advancing the following five points:

1. No person or group can commandeer a *superior* position in the structures of the church, or privileges that would allow forsaking the condition common to all, or even a responsibility that would establish a position *above* other persons and communities.[28] That is obvious and should be evident from a Christian point of view. But so many modes of functioning contradict this evident fact that for a long time it will still be necessary to repeat this principle and to claim full respect for it at the level of organization.

2. After having rejected a status of "superiority," it is still necessary to add that the fullness of the baptismal priesthood is

102

equally denied each time a person or a group situates itself *beside* it. There are theologies that invite one to this parallel course. How can one, for example, speak of "co-responsibility" as long as it is understood according to the logic and the present structure of clergy/laity relations? But, above all, there are properly ex-centric modes of being and of behavior also (with respect to the center that the baptismal priesthood should be) that perpetuate clericalism by renewing the caste spirit of those who walk beside the baptized.

3. Vatican II will not be respected in its deepest intentions as long as the ecclesiastical structures do not place the presbyterate and the episcopate *at the service* of the baptismal priesthood. It is quite evident that ecclesiastical life twenty years after Vatican II is still generally organized according to an opposed dynamic: it is the lay people who are at the service of the clerics and at the service of a pastoral practice defined essentially by the clerics.

4. It is not true that the presbyterate and the episcopate are at the service of the baptismal priesthood if priests and bishops set themselves up as a sort of untouchable a priori and, relying on this privilege that they have granted themselves, claim to be the *agent defining* the specific nature of their service. Persons and communities have to discover the possible meaning of this particular service that sacramentalizes the ordained ministry from the conditions of existence that history imposes on their being church.

5. The prerogatives of the baptismal priesthood are ridiculed each time that it is refused the *right* to the services for which priests and bishops have been ordained. What good is it, speaking of persons and communities, to affirm the *fullness* of their being and their responsibility if it is only to frustrate it immediately by shifting the exercise of the right elsewhere (toward the clergy in the present ecclesiastical structures). Persons and communities would then have full responsibility but without the right of exercising it!

103

A CHURCH OF THE BAPTIZED

Christian Decision and the Service of Ordained Ministers

For all practical purposes, we have learned to see the priest-mediator in a way that leaves the *believing decision* the room to accept or to reject the structural passivity of lay people. Nevertheless, is it not in this decision that Jesus Christ wishes to exist and to act as eternal mediator? Clericalism insults freedom-in-act where, as was said in the preceding chapter, the mediation of Jesus Christ must be situated. Whoever wishes to thwart clericalism (and to liberate lay people from the laity) finds here the full measure of his or her task, for it is here that the fate of Christian anthropology is decided. If one only considers the present state of clergy/laity relations, one can at least invite life and reflection to explore *three levels* that progressively open the field of freedom-in-act, of Christian decision, and of its responsibility.

1. On the first, most evident level, all the questions concerning the choice of ordained ministers, priests and bishops, arise.

It is quite evident that a certain reified conception of sacramental grace and, in particular, of the "priestly character" has deprived the Christian people of the very possibility of having anything to say about the choice of its ministers. Since everything takes place in a sort of immediacy between God and the minister who is ordained, where can the decision of lay people slip in? What leeway is given to the exercise of their responsibility? Candidates for the ministry respond to the urging of a "personally received inner call" and enter the seminary.[29] What does one do when they leave in order to effect a second "entry," this time into a restricted community, a parish, or a diocese? Because it was absent at the origin of the process, the decision of persons and communities is forced in the end to submit.

On the different levels of ecclesiastical organization, different reforms have been initiated concerning the choice of ordained ministers, and each of them would merit an attentive analysis. But how can one not wonder about their deeper meaning when one sees this long movement of the progressive restruc-

104

turing of the space come to die from the absolute power held by the pope in choosing the bishops? At the bottom, one tries to favor the broadest participation possible. But persons and communities are already condemned to having to struggle against another current which, with its source at the top, opposes the force of the opposite dynamic. As one sees more and more, this other current wishes to invade everything. It reserves for itself the power of spreading bit by bit over the whole of the ecclesiastical organization. By keeping for itself the final decision on the choice of each bishop, Rome assures itself in effect of control over the configuration of the bishops' conferences and ends by determining, in a more immediate manner than one is perhaps spontaneously led to believe, all the particular modes of ecclesiastical life. The life of the baptized ends by drowning in this current, so much does it concretely neutralize the very possibility of a responsible decision, both personal and communal.

2. This neutralization of the action of lay people shows very well the urgency of posing on a second level, in an even more fundamental sense, the problem of the being and the responsibility of believing decision. Clericalism will, in effect, continue to rage (and thus to constitute the laity) as long as this decision is not respected as the first and the last, in fact the only authority to which it falls to make the presbyterate and the episcopate exist *as an ecclesiastical service*. And this imperative must be understood in two ways. It first of all repeats what was already advanced above, namely, if the ordained ministry is necessary to the church, priests and bishops have *services to render* to which persons and communities have a right; it is thus the latter's place to decide if these services are being rendered effectively and if their right is being respected. But the field of decision is no longer sufficiently open to deprive clericalism of every hold. In effect, vocabulary and common meaning already tell to what extent the logic of "rendering services" can institute a relation of subject to object. One pole renders a service because it is rich in that in

105

A CHURCH OF THE BAPTIZED

which the other is poor. Priests and bishops would thus have the power to give to the laity what it does not have and can only receive from them. How can such a relation (especially in the "lack" it implies in the definition of the laity) be reconciled with the Christian confession of the baptismal priesthood as a full participation in the priesthood of Christ? To decide to make the presbyterate and the episcopate exist *as a service* of a church that has been restored to all means a *decentering* that is demanded of the ordained ministers and that *defines* their place in the church. Which authority will see that this decentering is effectively lived out? In the church of history, one sees no other than the persons and communities for whose benefit this decentering is to be exercised.

3. The third level carries the decision-making process by all so far that the invitation to enter upon it will be formulated in the mode of a question. The second chapter concluded that no person or community escapes from the responsibility of *making God exist* in history. With regard to the third chapter, it said that the task of mediating salvation itself is entrusted to all and that all in their humanity are charged with *making salvation exist*. In virtue of what, then, should the common responsibility cease to operate now that we have reached the field of sacramentality? Having arrived at this particular sacrament that is the ordained ministry, should personal and communal decision now abdicate? Hence the question: Do the episcopate and the presbyterate *exist* when believing consciousnesses are not *making them exist* as one particular sacrament in the service of the sacrament of the church? One surpasses here the order of the historical organization and of the concrete exercise of the presbyteral and episcopal service in order to ask about the very *existence* of the sacrament. With respect to the tradition of recent centuries, life and reflection are then confronted with thorny problems. Just think of the "indissolubility" of the "priestly character" and of our reified understanding of both this character and of its indissolubility.

Think further of a "sacramental grace" that would be directly and personally given to the clerics without any intervention of the communal freedom of lay people, etc. But do we do justice to the believing decision of the baptized when we give up on the way and do not arrive, when we tarry in putting the existence of the ministers back into the hands of believing persons and communities? For my part, I think that lay people will not leave the laity, that they will not exit from passivity, if the status of subject escapes them at the very last moment of the reappropriation, at the moment when the existence of the ordained minister should require the responsible intervention of their freedom-in-act.

5

The Mass

"An Outward Sign That Gives Grace"

The privileged place that Christians, and more particularly those of the Roman Catholic confession, accord to the celebration of the mass is well known. Furthermore, Vatican II reminds us: "Through the ministry of priests, the spiritual sacrifice of the faithful is made perfect in union with the sacrifice of Christ, the sole mediator. Through the hands of priests and in the name of the whole church, the Lord's sacrifice is offered in the eucharist in an unbloody and sacramental manner until he himself returns."[1] Our reflection thus passes to a fourth element that serves to define the structure of our contemporary religious mentality.

The text cited above connects the eucharist directly with the sacrifice of Christ the mediator. It also indicates the place of priests in the mass: it is "through their ministry," "through their hands," that "the spiritual sacrifice of the faithful is made perfect." Thus, in one short sentence, the council cannot help linking the eucharist directly with the two elements that the preceding chapters have just analyzed: priests and Christ. Noting these ties, one is entitled to ask: Does the understanding that one generally has of the eucharist only follow a bit further the exclusively deductive logic initiated previously? Put more bluntly, does eucharistic consummation of the Christian life, to take up the expression of Vatican II, also *consummate* the *activity* of clerics and the *passivity* of lay people? Attentive to the relations, our reflection does not question the eucharist in itself; it does not wish to deny its importance in Christian and ecclesial life. It only tries to understand the *ties* that the mass has maintained and still maintains with the global character of the religious landscape, it examines its relations with each of the other elements, and especially, and more immediately, it asks about the type of relations between clerics and lay people that the mass brings into play today.

It should have become evident that a fundamental question is now bearing on our reflection: What fate is reserved for the *freedom-in-act* of believing persons and communities? What do they have to *decide* in the celebration of the mass, if they have anything to decide at all? Once again, a valid answer requires consent to a twofold prior detour, the detour through the customary visions of the mass and that through the place that clerics and lay people occupy there respectively.

1.   A Sensible and Efficacious Mediation of the Action of Christ

We have learned, especially since Trent, that priests are ordained essentially for the celebration of the mass. Even in a book desiring the end of a clerical church, P. Guilmot writes: "The only point that really distinguishes the priest from the member of the faithful is that he has the power of celebrating the eucharist."[2] It is thus at the mass that priests exercise their power. But it goes without saying that a dynamic is exercised at the mass that organizes the whole of Christian and ecclesiastical life. If our reflection is interested now in the mass, in what is experienced there and in the ecclesiastical structure that it illustrates, what is at stake is nevertheless much higher. One finds there, in effect, an expression of the way in which Christians have learned to *manage the whole of their relations to the sacred.*

But although the entire question of Christian worship could be raised here, I shall speak above all of the mass and of the place that priests and lay people occupy there. Three successive steps will permit us to enter bit by bit into the work of questioning.

A CHURCH OF THE BAPTIZED

The Mass: An Act of God Through the Priests and Christ

It is no exaggeration to say that for the vast majority of people the mass *is only defined* by the top and *defines* the bottom. In other words, it is the object of the elements that precede it in the schema, and it is only their intervention that permits it to become in turn the subject of the bottom, of the church and of the world. Even a rapid examination of the relationships through which the mass enters into relation with each of the preceding elements reveals this clearly.

The mass is first of all defined by the priests. It is still common to identify "priest" and "celebrant of the mass": the priest, it is commonly said, is the one who *celebrates* the mass. This identification is not as innocent as it appears. As I said in the preceding chapter, it contributes to narrowing the field of operation of priests and bishops to an exaggerated degree. But this reduction constitutes the price to be paid in order to assure the latter of a monopoly on the entire ecclesiastical celebration of the faith.

To deny the innumerable and felicitous initiatives that have been taken to render eucharistic celebrations livelier and closer to people and their lives would be pure meanness. But are they sufficient? Furthermore, will this kind of adaptation ever be sufficient? Even today, Sunday mass in parish churches clearly reveals the structural game that continues to be brought into play: the lay people *attend* the mass that the priest *celebrates*. Everything turns around the altar which remains the domain of the priest and, by extension, of those whom he wishes to invite there. He remains the principal actor. While recognizing the initiatives taken for a greater "participation" of the faithful, is not the priest the *only* one who truly acts? In effect, when the moment that counts arrives, that of the consecration, lay persons inevitably remember what they have learned for a long time: the priest *consecrates*; he is pronouncing the words that are going to *make* the body and blood of Christ come into the bread and wine.[3]

110

THE MASS

What is the place of believing decision at this particular moment that is seen as decisive? What would those present, the crowd of lay persons, respond if they were asked how their freedom is then invited to intervene and to exercise what perhaps constitutes the most serious of its responsibilities? Without a doubt, for the vast majority the action takes place apart from them, and they can only receive as well as possible what is, as it were, the fruit of the priest's words, the consecrated bread and wine. As is still commonly said, they "receive communion" from the hands of the priests.

This indicates well enough how Christians read the consecration as a direct and immediate intervention of Christ. The dignity of the priest, in effect, arises from the power that Christ himself exercises and manifests each time that a priest celebrates mass. And the priests are the subjects of the celebration only insofar as Christ is constantly intervening to render them capable of it. I cited *Document IV* above because it says clearly what believers think and what their way of reading the action of Jesus Christ at the eucharist is.[4] This text links the priests directly with Christ who "by his ascension was withdrawn from the eyes" of his faithful ones. "Seated invisibly at the right hand of the Father," this eternal Christ wishes "to exercise his priesthood visibly in the church on earth and to render his own action manifest." If lay persons spontaneously read the bread and the wine as the *immediate* transcription of the body and blood of Christ, and if, regarding the priest, they directly see Christ himself, it is first of all because they wish to respond to what has been presented to them as the direct will of Christ, of the Christ of glory, "seated invisibly at the right hand of the Father." Who are the faithful to resist such a will? And, thus, who are they to seek anything else in the consecration than an exercise of the sovereign freedom of the glorious Christ? In any case, these questions have an inevitable counterpart: Does not such a view of things subjugate and alienate the human freedom of believers? It leaves them no other

111

A CHURCH OF THE BAPTIZED

decision than that of not intervening too much, of doing as little as possible, one could say, in order that the space necessary for an immediate coming of Christ in person might be cleared.

A recent text of John Paul II reflects on and maintains this vision which, one can already guess, is really harmful: "But one must not forget the primary office of priests, who have been consecrated by their ordination to represent Christ the priest: For this reason their hands, like their words and their will, have become the *direct instruments* of Christ."[5] The direct tie with Christ then permits a dramatic discourse on the hands of the priests, this "instrument" of the will of Christ: "To touch the holy species, to distribute it with their hands, is a privilege of ordained persons which indicates an active participation in the mystery of the eucharist." Would it be a caricature to add that this dramatization is possible insofar as the hands of the priests are seen as the hands *of God himself?* In any case, that is what Christians thought and still think. By touching and distributing the holy species, the priests touch and distribute that in which the God of Jesus Christ is immediately manifested. Their hands are thus a "direct instrument" of God himself. In them and through them, he begins salvation again and again. But in them and through them, one must add, God is revealed as an absolute of beginning: these hands would not be worthy of him if he did not intervene *each time* they consecrate in order to elevate them to this dignity. Thus, that is how, speaking of the hands of the priests, the mass is connected directly with God as an absolute beginning of everything but also, and above all, as an absolute of beginning.

Absence of the Church and of the World

The mass is thus defined by the priests, Christ, and God. There are two great absences in the dynamic set in motion by this common vision: the *church* and the *world*, i.e. the two elements that follow in the schema or, to put it more precisely, that the

THE MASS

schema situates *below* the mass. They are reduced to the condition of an object, do not act, and do not have to act.

Iconography always reveals the mental schemas that structure a religious mentality. Who does not remember those still recent times when the pictures, distributed on the occasion of a priestly ordination, showed the priest atop the steps that lead up to the altar, supremely alone or accompanied by children whose dress sufficed to assimilate them to the clergy? If the priests alone (perhaps accompanied by "servers") were not the church, the latter would be strangely absent from the action that was being accomplished. Think further of the proliferation of the so-called "private" masses without any "congregation" or, at best, with a server whom one strove to promote to a representative of all the baptized.

For a few decades, life and reflection have attempted to correct the most flagrant excesses. They have tried hard to rediscover the properly *communal* dimension of *every* celebration of the eucharist, even the most restricted one. It is a fact that the church has come a long way; one has to respect the immense efforts, entirely worthy of esteem, that have been approved to let communities (parishes, for example) participate in the celebrations of the eucharist. But are we not still a long way off? Is it certain that persons and communities understand the imperative that is being proposed, above and beyond the arrangements that are quite evidently necessary? If, in effect, decision has the importance we have said, and if the community is called to intervene in the celebration of the mass, the challenge does indeed seem to be the following: the mass will not exist as an act *of the church* as long as it is not *the act of a properly communal decision*, not the act of an isolated man, nor the celebration attended by an anonymous group of individuals, nor even the "participation" of all in the action of an individual (or of several, if one thinks of what is commonly called a "concelebration"), but the activity in which

A CHURCH OF THE BAPTIZED

the communal freedom of all and of each is mediated. In effect, recent initiatives are trying to educate believers by showing them how the eucharist *makes* the church community. And it is doubtless right to insist on this moment of the dynamic. But even today, it is not clear how the eucharist *is also made* by the community *as* a community.

Is the *world*, for its part, reduced to the condition of a passive object? Christians have not learned how they would have to intervene in the celebration of the mass.

Who has not heard this refrain taken up by more and more lay people: "I no longer go to mass; it no longer has any meaning for me, and I am bored there." Before crediting responsibility for this loss of fervor to the account of a laziness of faith, thus before moralizing the answers, would it not be well to listen at last to the structural question that this exodus is posing? If the mass has really become insignificant (without significance) for the lives of many lay people, it is first of all because these lives, which are inevitably lives *in the world*, do not enter into the (practical and theoretical) definition of the celebrations. In a word, what is called the *world*, as well as personal and communal existence at the very heart of this world, remains foreign to the production of the mass.

Once again, God knows the efforts that have been approved to render masses more lively. But these efforts have not clotted the hemorrhage, and the practice of religion continues to drop. One can bet that the defections will increase as long as the world, at the bottom, is not judged worthy of itself *defining* the eucharist also. Three indications will suffice to reveal the practical contempt that is harbored toward the world. The corner of *space* that lay people occupy matters little, be it the city or the country, the north of the rich or the third world, a disadvantaged quarter or an affluent suburb. Clerics continue to celebrate the mass in a way that is always identically the same. A second indication is that *time* is no longer taken seriously. There are indeed "liturgical

114

seasons," but they just constitute an intra-ecclesiastical time, the seasons "of the faith," a time proper to the liturgy. I should rather speak of that time which is the historical inscription of personal and collective geneses: Can a child celebrate like an adult? Can an experienced community simply repeat the ways of its beginnings? Can a world of the atomic age enter without further ado into a mold defined before the invention of printing? These first two indications point to a third: whether one is economically rich or poor, of one political party or another, involved in a given struggle of which one's neighbors are ignorant or to which they object, this entire *plurality* is drowned in a uniformity that levels everything out, in a eucharist that blesses everything and its opposite. Nevertheless, it is in this space-time and this plurality that the decision of lay people must be operative. Since it never exists in a chemically pure state, and, furthermore, since it is held at a distance in the production of the mass, how could this decision draw any (Christian and thus human profit) from a-historical, anonymous, uniform, and standardizing celebrations? The mass has ignored the world too much for the world not to be justified in ignoring it in turn.

"An Outward Sign That Gives Grace"
The monopoly exercised by the elements at the top and the absence of the bottom, of the human decision of believers, of that decision *as* the bottom conditions it—all these things question in the end the understanding that one generally forms of the *efficaciousness* of the eucharist. In fact, by means of this particular sacrament, the church is led today to reconsider the entire universe of its sacramental system. It has, in effect, to ask itself: Is there a *Christian* way of managing relationships with the sacred? And in particular, what is that way when it is a question of the mass? One thing is certain: the common mentality forms a properly *magical* conception of it. And it is clear that the customary presentation and common meaning of the mass as an "outward

A CHURCH OF THE BAPTIZED

sign giving grace" contributes to this.[6] Here one finds again (should one be surprised?) the harmful mediation that the preceding chapters have constantly run up against. Relying on what has already been said, four points will suffice to bring out the general set of problems in which the efficaciousness of the eucharist (and of the other sacraments) is experienced.

1. In the common understanding of sacramentality, everything always begins with a dichotomy. But why is that so? The phenomenon is incomprehensible if one does not first take account of the fact that Christian and ecclesiastical life is a *complex* reality. In the mystery of Easter, Jesus Christ simultaneously reveals the truth of God and the truth of humanity. Two poles have already been affirmed (*the divine and the human*) which forbid reducing the human writing of salvation to unidimensionality. They nevertheless offer a hold on the disjunctions (the "either-or's") which are literally expected to simplify life: either God or man, either the things above or those below, either prayer or action, either mysticism or involvement—one must either dedicate oneself to the things of salvation or apply oneself to the human liberation of a land that groans under the weight of innumerable oppressions, etc. The customary ways of situating the eucharist bring this drama into play. On the one hand, they affirm the *invisibility* of the sacrificial act that Christ exercises eternally, a definitive act that gives to the whole of history the ultimate meaning of its course, as, for example, *Document IV* said. But, on the other hand, persons and communities are really involved in a world from which they cannot detach themselves and which is the world of the *visible*. No doubt, the sacrifice of Christ and the (historical) one of Christians maintain ties that mutually compromise them. But, from the strict point of view of visibility, one could say they follow parallel, juxtaposed paths. That is why a *new* act of will of the risen Christ is necessary: "He wishes to exercise his priesthood visibly in the church on earth," said *Document IV* in order to justify the priesthood of priests.

116

THE MASS

That is already to presuppose that, even after Easter, the life of the Lord escapes the domain of the discernible and that believers cannot visibly express salvation in their visible activities that work for a transformation of the world. A *gap* has thus been dug here, a dichotomy has first been established, between the visible and the invisible. The a priori is the same for the other sacraments: baptism, for example, is necessary because a state of sin and a state of grace have been separated, so to speak; penance because one has to pass from the condition of sinner to that of forgiven, etc.

2. That is where the mediation of the Eucharist thus slips in. It fills the abyss between the visible and the invisible. It is an "outward sign": the act in which the invisible takes the initiative of revealing itself in a discernible manner, one visible in history. It is thus an objectified third term that comes to slip in between the two poles that, without it, would be irreconcilable. The same holds for all the other sacraments which are third terms: the priest slips in "between" Christ and the world in order to give Christ to the world; baptism takes the baptized in a state of sin to introduce him or her into the world of grace; penance produces forgiveness where sin had caused separation from God, etc.

3. Nevertheless, a twofold critique makes all these bridges collapse. At mass, the coming of the invisible into the visible cannot be said to be totally transparent in a way that would escape the opacity of things. As an "outward" sign that "gives grace," it is itself constrained to get lost in the sensible, in things (in this case, bread and wine) that, because they are things, do not reveal to the sensory gaze anything other than what they are: visibly speaking, the bread and wine always remain bread and wine. On the other hand, the mass (where, it is said, the entire process of rendering the invisible visible is exhausted and where, more generally, all historical existence finds the revelation of its salvific meaning) no longer expresses anything "visibly." It appears more and more to a greater and greater number of believers as withdrawn from what is

117

A CHURCH OF THE BAPTIZED

at stake in the world, from human challenges both personal and collective. It has lost all its human relevance for the Christian conduct of historical affairs.

4. But this customary understanding of sacramental efficacy reveals itself to be intolerable from a christological point of view. Even if it does not avow it explicitly, it presupposes that Jesus Christ has only more or less successfully managed salvation since it maintains a disjunction between the realities which, we confess, he has reconciled "once for all" (*satisfecit*, "he has done enough"). This type of efficaciousness destroys the unicity of the mediation of Jesus Christ by proposing an inadmissible mode of production: if, in effect, Christ is not always already at work where the sacraments arrogate to themselves the power of giving grace, *he will not be there either once they have been administered.* In order to correct the schemas of thought concerning the efficaciousness of the mass (and of the other sacraments), in order that believers may be liberated from magical mentalities, it is first of all necessary to reconsider the christological foundations that are given to this type of efficaciousness. I shall thus take up on another level a formula that has already been employed: the church always has the sacramental system that its christology deserves.

2. The Mass and Clergy/Laity Relationships

Has our reflection not just let itself be unduly distracted, getting lost in considerations that have nothing to do with the concrete ecclesiastical situation of the clergy and the laity? Sometimes, when the end has been reached, some detours reveal that they were in fact short-cuts. It is clear that the celebration of the sacraments, above all of the mass, constitutes the cultic foundation that is presently given to the organization of clergy/laity relationships. Just as worship organizes the relations of history to God, to the absoluteness of God, one can easily refer to it in order

118

to absolutize in return a particular structure. What better way is there of safeguarding the control of clerics over ecclesiastical life than to assure their absolute control over the eucharist?

I shall first take up a rather long passage from the letter of John Paul II cited above "on the mystery and the worship of the eucharist":

Through this fact, that is, as ministers of the holy eucharist, they have a primary responsibility for the sacred species, because it is a total responsibility: They offer the bread and wine, they consecrate it, and then distribute the sacred species to the participants in the assembly who wish to receive them. Deacons can only bring to the altar the offerings of the faithful and, once they have been consecrated by the priest, distribute them. How eloquent therefore, even if not of ancient custom, is the rite of the anointing of the hands in our Latin ordination, as though precisely for these hands a special grace and power of the Holy Spirit is necessary!

To touch the sacred species and to distribute them with their own hands is a privilege of the ordained, one which indicates an active participation in the ministry of the eucharist. It is obvious that the church can grant this faculty to those who are neither priests nor deacons, as is the case with acolytes in the exercise of their ministry, especially if they are destined for future ordination, or with other lay people who are chosen for this to meet a just need, but always after an adequate preparation (loc. cit.).

It would be difficult to express better, in such a short text, the present organization of eucharistic celebrations and thus, by extension, the respective place of clerics and lay people in the

A CHURCH OF THE BAPTIZED

entire life of the church. John Paul II makes himself a distributor of roles, he assigns to each group of Christians the place that is proper to it, but, above all, he clearly expresses the dynamics of their relations, how they can and should operate among themselves. Let us follow the movement of this text in reverse in order to see the role that is attributed to each of the actors.

1. The first actors encountered in this ascending movement are lay people. But are they truly actors? Do they act in the celebration of the eucharist? Concerning the offering of bread and wine as well as their consecration, things are clear: all action and all responsibility escape the laity. The distribution of communion thus remains. The principle of departure is then clear, it suffers no ambiguities: of themselves, lay persons can do nothing, not even in the distribution. How can this sort of ontological incapacity be justified? What does the pope say about the status of lay people? One will not be surprised to notice that John Paul cannot proceed otherwise than *by the negative* either. The sentence bearing explicitly on the distribution of communion introduces lay people, in effect, as persons "who are *neither* priests *nor* deacons." If necessary, they may attain to a certain status as active subject. But this would be by way of *concession* and not in the name of their own dignity and responsibility: "It is obvious that the church can grant this faculty to those who are neither priests nor deacons." But *who*, then, is this church that concedes? It is evidently identified with the priests, the bishops, and the pope, and it is the clerics who will "authorize" certain lay people to distribute communion after themselves, having determined that there is a "just need" and having defined the parameters of an "adequate preparation."

In actual practice, more and more parishes and dioceses are appealing today to lay persons to distribute communion. Some will say that this is not such a big thing, but with respect to an absolute power, and especially in the minds of those who hold it, this small intrusion cracks the entire edifice: a power ceases to be

120

THE MASS

absolute as soon as, in any moment of its activity, some power (however limited) escapes from it. The monopoly is quite simply denied. Furthermore, one can easily see that it is a monopoly that makes use of the mass to sacralize itself in order to exercise its power better over the totality of ecclesiastical life.

Many priests and bishops, and the pope himself, are calling lay people to the exercise of parish or diocesan responsibilities. But if they listen to John Paul II and adopt his ecclesiological logic, how can priests and bishops act otherwise than in the mode of concession? Many, in fact, lay people as well as priests and bishops, see there an entirely temporary necessity, a sort of momentary constraint imposed by the drop in the numbers of the clergy, a palliative to which we resort while waiting for priests to become more numerous and finally to reestablish the order of things. Another observable phenomenon is that priests and bishops issue their calls but, in doing so, impose norms of preparation modeled on what is required of the clergy. Lay people are always the losers in that game. Either the requirements seem inordinate, and they delay indefinitely in taking the place to which they are invited; or they enter into a curriculum that more or less subtly assimilates them to the clergy and clericalizes them; or, as soon as they have effectively exercised a certain power and shaken the monopoly, they are declared incapable and poorly prepared by the very ones who control the standards for an adequate preparation.

And nothing has yet been said about the relations of lay people to the Roman "authorities." I know of a diocese, for example, whose bishop has just been told by authorities several thousand miles away that he was wrong in declaring a "true necessity" and in entrusting true parish responsibilities to lay people. No doubt, the Roman authorities must know the concrete situation of the diocese and its own needs better than the persons and communities directly concerned! But let us end the recourse to illustrations, because the structural defect has been sufficiently indicated: the celebration of the mass is organized in

121

A CHURCH OF THE BAPTIZED

such a way that it *reflects* the concrete organization of the church and *sustains* relations where lay people are the object of clerics.

2. Between lay people and priests there is a shadowy region where poorly identified persons operate who can "touch the sacred species" and "distribute them with their own hands" while being neither entirely priests nor entirely lay people.

There are first of all the deacons who are closer to the priests but do not have, like the latter, the power of offering or of consecrating. Furthermore, they are no longer lay people exactly since they "can only bring to the altar the offerings of the faithful and, once they have been consecrated by the priest, distribute them." Then there are the acolytes, of whom one is careful to say at the outset that they are lay people, "neither priests nor deacons," but to whom a "ministry" is entrusted that does not seem to derive from their lay state. The pope, however, indicates the direction to be taken; he takes the trouble to indicate towards what side they are to be drawn: they are all the more apt to distribute communion as they are "destined" (let us note in passing that they do not destine themselves) "for future ordination."

The haziness that surrounds the operation of deacons and acolytes in eucharistic celebrations is not unrelated, it will be understood, to the impreciseness of their status in the organization of the church. But let us not speak of acolytes: those Christians who even know the cultic meaning of the word are rare, and, more important still, the vast majority probably does not even know that there are acolytes in the church. Vatican II, furthermore, wished to revive the diaconate. But the concrete life of parishes and dioceses does not know very well where to insert this new structural element whose value has been reasserted from above. As a consequence, how could one be surprised by the fact that, where there are ordained deacons, they are constantly obliged to fight against clericalizing urges? Their patterns of behavior, their language, and even their manner of dress show that some have already given in. But how many others, who are

122

THE MASS

no doubt more numerous, fear being snatched up for the purpose of a restrictive sacramentalization which they see has only a slight relationship with history and which would separate them from lay people, their life in the world, and their human work?

3. At the beginning of everything, there are the priests. The pope confers on them a responsibility for the eucharist that is "a primary responsibility for the sacred species, *because it is a total responsibility.*" This at least has the merit of being clear. As a justification of this total power, it appeals to the rite of the anointing of the hands. Of course, this rite "is not an ancient custom." But don't worry about that; it serves all the same to affirm "a special grace and power of the Holy Spirit" that, by consecrating the hands of the priests, links them directly to God and thus permits priests, in return, to use God to justify the totalitarianism of their power. In effect, God himself, in the Holy Spirit, guarantees the absolute control of priests over the production of the eucharist, from the offering of the bread and wine, through the consecration, to the distribution of communion. The priests have complete domination over the production of the mass, that "outward sign" that then "gives grace" to lay people. Such is the "privilege of the ordained," such is the measure of their responsibility. The only problem is that *nothing is left for lay people.*

And that is how, in the celebration of the mass, ecclesiastical relations are organized where the clergy controls everything, whereas lay people have no power and no responsibility. In his own way, John Paul II has just repeated that the laity *is defined only by the negative* and is ecclesiastically nothing.

3. Restoring Responsibility to Lay People

Christians maintain a magical conception of the mass because they receive it as a *sign* defined entirely outside their freedom in some place above, just as, in the world of things, the

123

A CHURCH OF THE BAPTIZED

driver encounters traffic signs that he has not made and that others have set up. But, in that case, have we not forgotten that the economy of grace is not reducible to the platitude of things? And how will the eucharist offer a word of faith that is humanly credible and liberating if it is efficacious only insofar as persons and communities agree to forsake their freedom and to submit passively to it? This already indicates the necessity of rethinking the place of lay people in the celebration of the mass as well as of the other sacraments. More precisely, do they have to intervene in the very production of the eucharist, and is their freedom in some way responsible for its efficacy?

Becoming the Subject of Eucharistic Celebrations Again
    Without its "human roots, the sacrament always runs the risk of being a plant 'grafted' onto everyday life."[7] In order that the eucharist not be experienced by lay people as the intrusion into their lives of a sign that has come to be grafted onto their lives as an extrinsic, heterogeneous, and alienating reality, they are called to find its human roots again. The preceding pages invite us to go further still: everyone must learn again that the eucharistic celebration radically (*radicaliter*: in its very roots, in its christological roots) *demands the intervention of his or her human freedom*. Drivers have no other choice than to obey the roadsigns; if they do not, they will pay the price of their disobedience. But this type of reception is quite poor in expressing the efficacy of the sacraments because it inevitably makes one fall again into reified mediation and condemns lay people to being nothing. In order to cease being lay people, Christians must thus rediscover that the eucharist does not exist for them if they do not take the (always historical) responsibility of making it exist. The contemporary reflection that promises finally to take the eucharist out of the alienating world of magic is the one that, imitating the ways of symbolic activity, restores to persons and communities their status as *active subject* of the eucharistic celebration. As a sacrament

THE MASS

of the passover of Jesus Christ, one of the historical *passages* that the church must live today if it wants to sacramentalize the great passage is that of persons and communities who will forsake their passivity in the face of the sacraments in order to become the active subject of them again.

Is this to say that the clerics lose all place at the mass? One thing is certain: they will lose it if they do not cease to be and to behave like clerics, if they block the passage to which I have just referred and refuse to become true servants of the responsibility of celebrating persons and communities. Furthermore, they have in fact already lost their old place where certain persons and communities have begun to forsake the schemas of the magical mentality. Another ecclesiastical logic has been instituted that is transforming the organization of life. According to this new logic, no one can welcome the definers of the sign, its mediators, and its controllers any longer since the "sign" itself, the sacrament as a sign, and its relations with that existence and passivity in which it stifles life and its geneses have been rejected.[8] The sign as reified mediation appeals in vain to an "action of God" in order to absolutize itself, and the priest mediators buttress their power on an alleged divine will in vain. But that does nothing because Jesus Christ saves us from these totalitarianisms of the sign and of its mediators when he puts salvation into the hands of believers again, when he entrusts it to their freedom in act and their decision.

But it is necessary to give a better foundation to this reversal of perspectives, at least to suggest how, in the name of their faith, all must be responsible for the eucharist and all the sacraments. The three following points open some paths to this work of explicitation.

Fully Responsible for the Eucharist
By confessing the fullness of their baptismal priesthood, all confess at the same time the measure, which is literally without

125

A CHURCH OF THE BAPTIZED

measure, of the responsibility that Jesus Christ entrusts to their lives in history.

All that, of course, is indeed in the nature of the confession; it refers to the ineffable element of the faith and thus cannot be expressed in humanly clear terms: if it is a *fullness*, the baptismal priesthood will always escape from those ventures that try to "contain" it, so to speak. One will thus speak of it as a utopia. But it is even more correct to refer here to the Christian hope in order to express the realism of this utopia, the always possible historical encounter of salvation with limits and even with sin. The strength of hope is that it springs from sources too deep ever to die when the hopes defined by the intellect and the will have died. But its poverty is also a fragility that renders it easily recoverable. And one aspect of its fragility is that one way of understanding the mass has indeed recovered it: this understanding claims to have subtracted the hoping existence from the ineffable since it presents the mass as a humanly clear word (an *"outward sign"*) that "gives grace" and thus makes salvation exist immediately in human freedom.

"I am no longer a practicing Catholic," people often say who no longer attend Sunday mass, so much has the mass been made to coincide with the entire practice of Catholic life. But why has Catholic worship gone to take refuge in the church and particularly in the mass that is celebrated there? And why, at the same time as this cultic exodus, has the hope of Christian freedom ceased to be translated into historical projects of liberation? Contraries are of the same genus. When persons and communities abdicate their full responsibility in the eucharistic celebration, when they rely on the mass as an outward sign that is going to give grace in their place, so to speak, they displace the true place of Christian worship, which is the history of persons and collectivities, and, having lost their *full* responsibility restored in Jesus Christ, they cease at the same time to make themselves responsible for humanity.

126

THE MASS

Christians will not, however, rediscover the full measure of their responsibility for the eucharist without also finding their responsibility again in the face of those who defined the totality of the celebration of the mass. Priests and bishops, without excluding the pope, should at least expect that much when they have the generosity (with quite correct intentions, by the way) to restore the church to the responsibility of all. In the very process in which lay persons are going to take this responsibility and cease being lay persons, they are going to force the priests, the bishops, and the pope to cease being and behaving like clerics. Furthermore, as is already happening, this is going to take place in small and fragile experiences. But, in spite of their fragility, these experiences are already illustrating the unavoidable challenge to which all those who are concerned to convert the present state of clergy/laity relations must consent.

History and Eucharist

Christians are thus invited to liberate Christian worship from an understanding of the mass that holds it prisoner. But in virtue of what are we obliged to respond to this invitation and, above all, what direction should we take in order to convert the customary visions of the mass? It is necessary to ask here about the conditions of possibility for a worship that is truly Christian and thus about the relationships that the eucharist maintains with this worship.

It is not at all sufficient to confess a total responsibility of believers if one understands thereby that this responsibility operates in a vacuum, in an autonomous world (even if it is the world of "faith") that would not be subjected to the constraints of an existence in history. Participation in the mystery of Jesus Christ baptizes persons and communities into Easter, into the passage, and Christian worship is only experienced in these historical passages, both personal and collective, to which the urgencies of the present and the particularities of the places that we inhabit

127

A CHURCH OF THE BAPTIZED

and that inhabit us invite us. In order for history to be the history of a truly Christian worship, believing freedom must respond to a double imperative. First of all, it has the mission of liberating Jesus Christ, not by approaching the world to apply there its little catechism, its pre-defined rules, or a code that would pre-contain the truth of this world, but rather by the dynamics of its own hope, by serving to *open* the world to the dimensions of the gift of salvation that is offered to it, a gift that reminds it to what extent it only has historical meaning itself when it is a *process of liberation and a genesis of freedom*. Hence the second imperative: there simply is no Christian worship where individuals and collectivities are not *working* toward an *historical* liberation of the world. Are we Christians if, believing in the divine sonship and a universal brotherhood, we are not working to liberate concrete situations where the dignity and the responsibility of all, their vocation as sons or daughters of God and as universal brothers or sisters, are not recognized and at times are even denied? It would be as well to say that, in order to be Christian, worship must first recognize the world, its limits, and even its sin as one of its *conditions of possibility*, i.e. that without which worship is not even possible from a Christian point of view.

But can one believe that while conserving the customary relationships with the mass and, in particular, without healing it of its a-historicity? The latter is doubly harmful. It preserves the mass from every contagion by subtracting it from the risks that the world (including limits and sin) would have it run, but does so at the price of a fall into historical irrelevance and insignificance. On the other hand, maintaining the mass in the arrogance of its isolation forbids the eucharistic meaning of the world itself to be experienced, expressed, and celebrated. Lay people are thus led to subvert their relations to the mass from the moment that they see that the worship pleasing to the God of Jesus Christ is a fullness of life that is the genesis of freedom. The mass is not condemned to disappearing by the simple fact that one refuses to

THE MASS

consider it after the manner of things, and its efficacy is not denied because one does not allow oneself to live it according to the dynamics of physical causality. On the contrary, persons and communities will no doubt rediscover it for what it should never have ceased to be: a eucharist, the sacramental celebration of *all* life, of that which Jesus Christ gives us to live when, fully inhabiting our world, we all work for its total liberation. The mass becomes significant again, it makes sense and gives meaning, when believers withdraw its monopoly on worship in favor of the sole place that is worthy of Christian worship: the world and its history.

A similar subversion of their relationships with worship and with the eucharist inevitably leads lay people to subvert their relations to the clergy also. To put it clearly, as soon as they learn to be the subject of the eucharist, they have already entered into a process where they cease being lay people cultically defined by the negative. Having become agents again of the true Christian worship in the world, how could they content themselves with being "acted upon" by the mass and those who control it? They have been reconciled with human history as the place of worship, they are rediscovering themselves as responsible for the eucharistic celebration, and thus are exploding the old structures of their relationships with the clergy. Priests and bishops often experience this new appropriation on the part of lay people as a despoilment of their own being. But, no doubt, this disappropriation perhaps constitutes a piece of good fortune for them: only lay people who have ceased being lay people and communities that have finally got rid of clerics will be able to help the priests, the bishops, and the pope to deliver themselves from clerical structures that are still stifling their lives.

The Eucharist and the Human Decision of Believers

The passivity of lay people at the mass finds its justification in a presupposition that the Christian faith condemns. In speak-

129

A CHURCH OF THE BAPTIZED

ing of the mediation of Jesus Christ and of the new relationships that it permits between God and human history, the fate of salvation was, in effect, entrusted to the freedom-in-act of believers, to their human ability and responsibility to *decide*. The confession of Jesus Christ is thus not without a double refusal concerning the mass. The latter is not an exercise freed from all constraint and cut off from history, to which there is an invitation when it is placed above the world and human freedom. Furthermore, how is one to accept that the action of faith should be obliged to go to meet a closed world, one impervious to every wager of faith in favor of the God of Jesus Christ, and thus entirely resistant to the meaning of salvation that the eucharist celebrates? In order to counter these two ways of paralyzing the historical existence of persons and communities, there is no other way than that which restores worship, and thus its celebration at the eucharist, to the *human decision*, both personal and communal, of the baptized.

This is indeed the first and last authority that can convert the present relationships of lay people to the mass. The passover of Jesus Christ so restores their human freedom to believers that the worship pleasing to the God of Jesus Christ is now experienced in the never clear and always ambiguous historical decisions that try to change something in the present state of the world. Does the mass "give grace"? One thing is certain: the Christian answer to this question will continue to elude those who are content with a passive reception of communion. Bread and wine do not deliver the body and blood of Jesus Christ magically nor the freedom that is assured in the body that is given and the blood that is poured out. On the contrary, it is always necessary, especially at those numerous moments when belief is not self-evident, for all to intervene in order to *decide* to read the bread and the wine as the sacrament of Easter.[9]

Reified mediation leads to experiencing the mass as a properly magical act. But each time that this is the case the clerics are

130

THE MASS

forced (or force themselves) to live and behave as magicians, as men who make God come without the personal and communal freedom of lay people being part of this coming. Quite evidently, the rediscovery of baptismal dignity and the sole fact of restoring responsibility for the eucharist to the decision of all explode the present structure of clergy/laity relationships. In effect, it forbids living and thinking of historical relationships in which the clergy have control of worship and are everything in the eucharistic celebration, standing above lay people who content themselves with attending and receiving. As subjects of the eucharist because they are in their decisions historical subjects of the new worship instituted in the passover of Jesus Christ, persons and communities are learning that the eucharistic consummation of ecclesiastical life is also a sacramental consummation of their being church and of their total responsibility for the life of the church.

6

The Church

From a Clerical Church to a Church of Communion?

God through *Christ* gives to the *priests* a power over the *mass*. These are the first four poles that I presented in the first chapter in order to describe the contemporary religious mentality. The exposition then continued with the following statement: at the mass, the church fully realizes its nature as a sacrament of Christian salvation. We thus come to a fifth element of the religious landscape of Christians today, *the church*.

I could adopt for this chapter the same procedure as in the preceding chapters. It would first be a question of seeing how the elements at the top (God, Christ, priests, and mass) *define* the church, how they are the subjects that tell its truth, and how a direct intervention of these elements is necessary in order for it to act in the world. On the other hand, it would be equally necessary to look at its relations with the bottom, with the world. This second look would then bring out to what extent the church, as directly elevated by the top to the status of an active subject, has considered and still considers the world as a passive object whose truth is so *defined* by it that it has no other choice than to turn to the church in order to receive from it its meaning of salvation and, further, its human meaning pure and simple.

Nevertheless, I shall take another path in speaking of our general conceptions of the church. Two things justify my doing so. In the first place, four chapters have certainly sufficed to illustrate the method employed until now, to indicate the direction of a process that each one can pursue, and even to suggest the possible content that this analysis would deliver. Further-

THE CHURCH

more, I hope that the preceding chapters have sufficiently told the importance of the *passage* in the Christian faith to justify me in approaching the church from this angle. Because the Easter passage of Jesus Christ constitutes the mediating act into which we are baptized, an anthropology is only Christian if it tries to account for the Christian vocation to the passage, to nomadism. The logic thus forces us to conclude that if the church is the sacrament of such a mediator, if it exists in history through and for those beings dedicated to the passage, *it has no other way to sacramentalize salvation than in and through those historical passages that it is constantly called to live.* That is how I should like to approach the questions of ecclesiastical life and structure.

But rather than discoursing theoretically on the church and its passages, rather than saying what a church "of the passage" should ideally be, I wish to look at what is and, faithful to the perspectives assumed from the beginning, to ask about the present state of things.

In the present state of things, I notice first of all that many persons (lay people as well as clerics) do not even think that the church is invited to any historical passage at all. For them, things are thus clear, and what I am going to say is absurd from a Christian point of view. My questions should thus only interest the persons and communities who read in Jesus Christ the call to a necessary passage. What I then find concerning the church can be formulated very generally in the following way: the church must pass today *from the uniformity of a clerico-pyramidal church to a church of communion.*

That is why I shall approach the mystery of the church by speaking of its *unity*. To what does the term "unity" refer? In its general sense, unity merely means the "character of what is one *in any one of its meanings.*"[1] All that the word "unity" means is that a reality is simply *one*. But the words in italics underline a capital point: in itself, unity is *undifferentiated*, it does not account for the differences that cause the several forms of unity. For

133

A CHURCH OF THE BAPTIZED

example, it equally designates the unity of a chair, of a married couple, of a dictatorship or a democracy, etc. Each of these realities is "one," but it would easily be agreed that all are not understood according to the same mode of unity. Hence the importance, when it is a question of *ecclesiastical* unity, of describing it from a Christian point of view. It is on this task of clarification that I wish to dwell a bit.

Thus, before reflecting on the future of the laity in a church of the passage, even before bringing out the structure of the clergy/laity relationships implied in our contemporary understanding of the ecclesiastical passage, I shall ask about the latter, the passage that ecclesiastical unity is invited to experience, such as it is commonly experienced today. More precisely, the question that I bring is the following: Is it indeed necessary to pass *from* uniformity *to* communion today? As one can see, it is once again the question that interests me, or the way, which tends to be generalized, in which one is led to present the passage.

1.   Passing from the Uniformity of Clericalism to Communion?

On the left and on the right, almost everywhere that I encounter people and communities to whom it appears clear that the church is driven today to experience a fundamental passage, the point of departure seems clear: the church must forsake its pyramidal organization. More concretely still, that means getting rid once and for all of a clericalism that confuses *unity* and *uniformity*. The point of arrival seems equally evident, for it is necessary in order finally to attain a church of *communion*. Nevertheless, are things really so clear and the terms of the passage so evident?

At least one thing can be guessed: it is not sufficient to *identify* in perfect clarity *what* the church should forsake (here: clericalism and its propensity to standardize everything) and *what* it should attain (here: communion). In effect, such a simplistic view of the passage lets it be understood that one day the church will finally be able to rest, to cease passing, once it has left the point of departure for good and attained the point of arrival forever, when clericalism has died and communion is finally experienced. Who does not see the impasse to which this rapid view of things leads? When the passage has been effected and finally accomplished, what will remain to get the church going again and to remind it of its nomadic *nature?* Will it then cease having to sacramentalize by its own passages the great passage of Easter? Satisfied and sated, having arrived, and having nothing more to respond to the calls of anyone anywhere, movement and progress will no longer be an integral part of its definition.

It would be as well to say clearly what I think: there are properly ideological ways of thinking of both uniformity and communion. Since the notion of ideology is an important one in this chapter, I shall first take the time to specify the meaning that I am giving to it here. With K. Rahner, I shall first situate it in this way: ideology is "an erroneous and false system incompatible with the correct interpretation of the real. . . . Ideology is essentially distinguished, however, from simple error. Whereas the latter remains *open* in principle, ideology implies a decision to constitute itself as a closed system sufficient unto itself. If one confines oneself to the customary terminology, it is thus proper to ideology to close itself to the whole of the real in order to give a partial aspect of it the coefficient of an absolute. But it is necessary to complete this abstract description of the nature of ideology. Since the latter claims, in effect, the adherence of men, one is on the terrain of action, and ideology takes on a practical flavor: it inspires a politics, and in the end it becomes the supreme regulator of the general life of a society."[2] This context permits us to understand the entire range of the definition of ideology that Rahner then borrows from Lauth and that I am here making mine for the purpose of the analysis that I intend to pursue:

A CHURCH OF THE BAPTIZED

ideology is a "pseudo-scientific interpretation of the real in the service of a political (in the broad sense of the word) design with the purpose of legitimating it after the fact."[3]

Having clarified this, I submit that there are ideologies of uniformity and of community that entail *alienations* in the point of departure or the point of arrival, backward and forward looks that claim to be liberating but already bear death because they substitute dreams for life, dreams that have no relationship with history. That lay people are not vaccinated against ideology is evident. But since clericalism founds its power on an a priori that it controls itself, the structure of the church tends to transform clerics into ideologues. That is what I wish to explain.

Forsaking the Uniformity of Clericalism?

With respect to what I should call alienation in the point of departure (or *the ideology of uniformity*), it seems to me that the analysis must discern *three ways* of considering uniformity, three ideologies that block the passage, that forbid it a priori. It is thus important, even vitally so, to look attentively at each one of these three forms, even if ultimately these three sin by a vice that is common to them all.

1. The first ideology consists in thinking and saying that *the uniformity of clericalism is a "thing of the past"* (but especially in acting accordingly).

One pretends here that the church has already left behind the uniformity and the oppression that it inflicted on life. A number of illustrations will indicate the topicality of this vision. For many, for example, Vatican II has done a good deal of housecleaning here. Thanks to its proposals for communion, thanks above all to the pastoral initiatives to which the council gave rise, uniformity is now no longer possible.[4] Why did the extraordinary synod of 1986 (on "The Church Twenty Years After Vatican II") frighten so many Christian persons and communities if not because many feared that what they had considered a

THE CHURCH

definitive acquisition was being threatened? The uniformity that had been classified as being among the "things of the past" suddenly became a very present threat. Another illustration: because they have the good fortune (more accurately: the grace) of living in an ecclesiastical community that makes a place for personal and communal originality, many let it be understood that everything is now settled forever and project a judgment on the whole church that they do not even perceive as being totally idealistic. I still remember those Christians who, because they worked in a parish whose priest "left lay people much initiative" (as they said), were incapable of experiencing uniformity as a *present* threat, a threat that is presently offering a challenge to the church. They were greatly disillusioned the day the bishop took the initiative of changing the parish priest! Think further of young people. How many of my students accuse me of unearthing quite old cadavers when I attempt to integrate in ecclesiology the very possibility of uniformity and of its faithful companion, clericalism. "We haven't experienced that. That was perhaps true of the church thirty or forty years ago, but today . . ." But, once their studies are finished and they are grappling with concrete ecclesiastical commitments, how many confess to me (with sadness or anger) their disenchantment before the real state of the church and its organization? How many confess that an apathy lies in wait for them proportionate to the idealism of the unrealistic dreams on which they fed and which have just collapsed?

I could multiply illustrations without end. Those that I have advanced no doubt suffice to make this much understood: it is pure ideology to enclose clericalism and uniformity in a past moment, in a moment of the past, for the church would then no longer have to effect a passage today, to convert itself, *for lack of a place from which to begin the passage.*

2. The rejection of this idealism forces us to conjugate clericalism in the present. The critique of the ideology of conformity is not for all that finished. On the contrary! Who has not

137

A CHURCH OF THE BAPTIZED

noticed that phenomenon which, for my part, I never cease to observe: it is gladly admitted that the church continues to be paralyzed by uniformity, that clericalism prevents it from effecting the passage to a true communion, but both clericalism as well as its aims to standardize *are transferred outside oneself, outside one's own person or one's own ecclesiastical community.* At bottom, there is indeed a fundamental defect, but it is always a defect for which "the others" are responsible.

Such is, in my opinion, the most common form of a harmful ideology. It is fatal for every experience of church, even and above all when it appeals to a great desire of bringing a church of the passage into existence in order to justify itself. One then lets it be understood that the church would be so much more alive if "the others" did not imprison it in uniformity.

One will have recognized a very widespread attitude among lay people. They have suffered so much from clerics who, under the pretext of the divine will, imposed their own designs, which, for all that, were quite "human." How can one be surprised, then, that uniformity has become for the majority of lay persons an affair of the clergy, a malady proper to the priests, the bishop, and the pope? But do the clerics have a monopoly on the vice of uniformity? A few years ago I made the rounds of a diocese that wanted to raise the question of the church. At each place we had the same experience. At the beginning of the progression, clericalism was for the majority of the participants the affair of vicars, of parish priests, or of the bishop. But the more things progressed, the more the question shifted. I remember one man in particular who, at the end of two days, formulated his realization more or less in this way: "I gladly accuse my priest or my bishop of clericalism. But I am realizing to what extent I behave like a cleric in my relations with my children and my students by not sufficiently resisting the temptation to impose my way of seeing on them and thus by willing to standardize their ways of understanding and acting."

THE CHURCH

It is self-evident that clerics do not, for all that, escape this form of pathology. Those who transfer the harmful game of standardization outside themselves are many. What, for example, is in play beneath the almost automatic suspicion manifested by priests, bishops, and the pope as soon as lay people deeply involve themselves with a political option? Why is there this insistence of the pope in particular to remind them that "such" an option is not that "of the church" as soon as lay people exercise an option that differs from the "official" position of the hierarchy? Is it not because one automatically suspects lay people who commit themselves a bit seriously of authoritarianism and attributes to them the intention of standardizing the church? The impression is thus given that the more lay people have clear and precise political options the more they should be automatically suspected of wanting to control everything and to impose their personal opinions on others. In a parallel fashion, the clergy is then presented as guaranteeing the "communion of faith." Because they have given themselves the responsibility for this communion, the priests, the bishops, and the pope are not tempted to standardize the faith by losing it in "one" particular choice (a political one, for example). What illusions!

When one transfers uniformity outside oneself, it is the church that is once again blocked in its vocation to passage. How can I affirm, on the one hand, that I am church and that the church is today invited to pass from uniformity to communion when, in the same breath, I transfer uniformity outside myself, that point of departure for the ecclesiastical passage? One should be a bit logical with oneself! Either each person and each community is church, and each one is responsible for leaving the point of departure (uniformity) and passing to communion, or uniformity is operative "outside" where passage and conversion are then the affair "of the others." But it is also into the hands of the others that the church has been abandoned!

3. Though refusing to consider clericalism a thing of the

139

A CHURCH OF THE BAPTIZED

past, have we sufficiently clarified what is generally presented as the "point of departure" of the passage that the church is supposed to live once tendencies to standardization have been brought back home to each one of us? I rather believe that a third level of blockage exists where a third ideology is operative, one perhaps more subtle than the first two but not less perverse. It consists in thinking that *we could possibly be liberated during the time of history from that which permits clericalism, i.e. the tendency to standardize life.*

I shall say it clearly: if clericalism has such a hard life, it is because uniformity answers to a deep *need of security.* God is not too disturbing as long as one pushes him up above or entrenches him behind a transcendence that isolates him from our lives. But, answering to the logic of the Christian faith, what becomes of God as soon as one seeks him here below? What face does God take on when we respect the invitation of Jesus Christ and regard our lives, our personal and collective responsibilities, as *the* place of the revelation of God? It was perhaps thought that the world with its limits and the challenge it issues to our responsible decisions was disturbing. But now it is God himself who in Jesus Christ disturbs us. Who is God? Where is he? What is his desire for us?

In effect, history is far from being the perfect reflection of an absolute transcendence. It offers its share of happiness, the joys of love, and treasures of generosity. In short, it makes a gift of everything that, in the balance sheet of our lives, we spontaneously enter in the credit column. But that which is to be found in the debit column obstinately unfolds in history also. History recalls implacable limits, repeats again and again that there is egoism in the world, that death is already inscribed in our bodies since, from birth, the human being is already old enough to die. Who is God when one must go to meet him in death and in all the anticipated deaths that each one has to experience almost daily? God is evidently less disturbing, he reassures or calms our

THE CHURCH

apprehensions, if he at least is not lost in our deaths. It is thus not without reason that, in spite of what Jesus Christ wishes to teach us, all of us are led to condemn God to exile. For then this reassuring security endures as a haven of peace to which one can return when history becomes threatening.

But there is another field where persons and collectivities experience the same drama, and it is that of *unity*. Everyone has probably experienced and still experiences intense moments of communion. The others (more precisely: a given other or group) are then so close that relations with them are experienced as an unbroken whole. Each one feels such a deep accord with the others that they are like a part of oneself and that, at certain moments of grace, even words become useless. Unfortunately, there is also difference! There are those persons and groups outside the warmth of the hearth with whom relations are rather cold. Their mere physical presence reminds one that "the unbroken whole" *is not the whole*. If Jesus invites us to live with them also, it will be necessary to have much time and patience, to talk much without being sure of ever being understood, to brush constantly against the risk of division. Further, this risk of division becomes a part of life when one realizes to what extent no one has the right to colonize others. But what becomes of God when it is there that he must be sought? And what better outward show is there before the threat of division than to standardize it itself? God gives infinitely more reassurance and security when one attributes to him the traits defined by the little catechism or when, mouthing the norms that clearly say what God is, nothing remains for history but the leisure of *conformity*, the leisure of conforming to what was defined as being "of God." One gladly accuses of totalitarianism the persons or the (political among other) organizations who deny God in order better to establish their absolute will to control. But does one see that there is another totalitarianism, one perhaps worse than the first, that which *uses God* to standardize life? That is the ultimate founda-

141

tion that the ecclesiastical power of clerics always gives itself. But one will also understand that, in the last analysis, uniformity will remain attractive as long as history pushes the church to go in search of plurality, that pocket of resistance that forbids it to think of its communion after the manner of a fusion and thus to confuse *unity* and *uni-formity*.

If such is indeed the case, the church *will never be delivered* from the risks of standardization and clericalism. To think the contrary, merely to hope that someday it will be different, is to sink into alienation, to fall asleep in a dream, a dream that perhaps distracts one from harsh reality but that also prevents one from seeing that *the unity of the church will always remain to be built*. Will the church one day escape the risks of a standardization of personal and collective lives? In other words, will it ever leave what is presented as the "point of departure" of its passage?

It will always have to set out again and again if it is the case that clericalism is so deeply rooted in it as I have tried to say. It will thus not undertake the journey toward communion when it has the leisure of doing so at the moments of greatest repose or of greatest generosity. It is its nature to be on the march, and nomadism is part of its definition. In short, the church *only exists when it is passing* from a standardizing clericalism to communion, and, in spite of our dreams that it be otherwise, it will always exist this way if it really wishes to be the sacrament of *the passover* of Jesus Christ.

Passing to Communion?

As one will have guessed, communion is what poses the question in a peculiar way about the term of the passage, about what tends to be presented as the point of arrival. Personally, I see certain ways of speaking and doing, certain proposals for the passage to communion, that for all practical purposes are an invitation to pass into a void!

The term "communion" translates the Greek word *koinonia*.

THE CHURCH

It expresses a twofold content of the Christian faith, namely, it "expresses in the New Testament *the relations of the Christian with the true God* revealed by Jesus and *those of Christians among themselves.*"[5] Communion is thus of the nature of the faith, of the Christian creed. But ideology can so distort it that it falsifies the point of departure. Certain visions, in effect, seem to me quite idealistic. They thus solicit the vigilance of reflection: to let oneself be dragged into their shimmer is perhaps to yield very concretely to certain appetites for domination that, even if they do not take the paths of old, are no less dangerous for the life of the church. It is not an exaggerated concern for symmetry that makes me find the number "three" again and urges me to speak once more of a triple ideology. These three forms present an alienating communion, a communion that, rather than inviting the church to passage and conversion, renders it insignificant as an historical reality by preventing it from being itself on the march in history.

1. A first form of alienation is to situate the existence of communion *beyond the term of history*. This is unfortunately a customary approach, one still widespread in my opinion, that pushes communion toward eternity, it then being understood that eternity is what begins after death when human beings finally escape the inexorable flow of time.[6] Because they are the heirs of a mentality for which eschatology is so crudely thought of in its relationships with history, a mentality that transfers "true life" beyond the last moment of their time, Christians today have evidently not learned to situate the ecclesiastical communion in the *here and now*. They continue to think that their true homeland is elsewhere and for later, and it will remain for later as long as the history of their human existence is not closed.

What can we do while waiting, if not just *wait?* In the Christian faith, there is (and should be) waiting indeed. But it is a waiting that is the very opposite of a wait-and-see-policy, a waiting that believes too much in an already given salvation and

143

A CHURCH OF THE BAPTIZED

freedom to be satisfied with the present state of the unity of the human race and to wait passively for some miracle to heal our weariness of life. It thus becomes an active waiting, it translates into a commitment to the historical liberation of a communion that wishes to gather together the men and women of our world. For its part, our customary wait-and-see-policy no longer grasps what are called "the last things" as what gives a future *to our today* and thus as a *present* reality. It is urgently necessary for the communion of faith to be brought back home to the present. That is the condition for every person and community (from the smallest to the largest), far from ever being satisfied with the present state of their unity, constantly to take up anew the building of their ecclesiastical cohesion, the construction of the unity of the church.

2. The second form of ideology consists in *conjugating* the historical existence of communion *in the future*. Of course, it will be said or understood that communion is historically possible and thus should not be transferred beyond time. But in the face of what the church shows us today, the historical existence of communion is for the future, for tomorrow or thereafter.

In effect, whatever the form of common life under consideration, the present state of ecclesiastical unity evidently appears limited, even filled with egoism and sin. That seems evident when one considers relations and history in the long run: the universal church is so pulled by all sorts of tensions and torn by conflicts, and its history offers the spectacle of so many fatal divisions! Could communion be there? Could that be the fraternal family of the sons and daughters of God? On a smaller scale, parishes and dioceses, particularly today, are far from being models of an unbroken fusion. Even the most restricted communities constantly live in the fear of a possible division. The most difficult ecclesiastical experience I have ever had in this respect was that of a very small community: the weekly meetings, in effect, heightened our consciousness of the fact that our faith and our

144

THE CHURCH

words as believers are never identically the same. Noticing this omnipresence of limits and the egoism that sometimes turns plurality into division, how can one continue to conjugate the existence of communion in the present? The simple solution is to drown oneself in the future: communion will exist *the day that*, thanks to sustained efforts and incessant purification, the cohesion of the church will perfectly reflect the great family that was merited in the passover of Jesus Christ. It would be as well to say that the church will be the sacrament of its Lord *once* it has gotten rid of its limits and of all the weight of sin that lies within it.

But a triple critique must be raised against this constant postponement. The first one concerns precisely the constancy of the postponement. If the Christian faith confesses the marriage of God with history insofar as this history is not written with any other than human words, and even with words of sin, the historical existence of communion will *always* be postponed to later. Why, then, should one continue to confess the church as a sacrament of Christian communion? Why should one take the responsibility for ecclesiastical life upon oneself? Since it is always for tomorrow or thereafter, the church rather becomes the sacrament of an indefinite frustration. A dynamic we have already encountered is reborn with a new face: we no sooner think we have come closer to communion through victory over certain limits when others present themselves and postpone the existence of true ecclesiastical life until later. The second critique better expresses the alienation that the church then nourishes. Such a church is not, in effect, *for us* and never can be during the time of history. Persons and collectivities do not *have* limits from which they could dream of being delivered one day. They *are* limits and will remain so as long as space-time is their natural habitat. The alienation to which postponing ecclesiastical communion until the future logically condemns us is that the church will not exist as the sacrament of Jesus Christ, it will not exist for us, until the day when it will no longer be necessary because we will no longer

A CHURCH OF THE BAPTIZED

be! By waiting, Christians exhaust themselves in the pursuit of an alienating dream. The latter perhaps distracts one from the harshness of the present, but it also serves as a comfortable alibi for our absences from history and the struggles that constitute it. Even worse, perhaps, such a church cannot be *for us*. This third critique expresses another facet of alienation in the future. How is one to believe that all persons and communities are *the subject* of the church when one notices the limits of each and, in spite of all the good will imaginable, none can hope someday to be the perfect model of Christian communion? One can guess what a large door has just been opened: during this time, when each one is running after the unattainable, the field is open for all kinds of appropriation, and certain ones are quick to seize what unceasingly escapes the others. Clericalism has deceitfully slipped into this space of the present that the future has emptied, this terrain left vacant by all those who have confused Christian hope and human hopes.

3. It is said that the church must pass from a standardizing clericalism to the fullness of communion. But where should its communion be situated if it cannot be postponed beyond history or until after the moments in which we are always living? It is necessary to conjugate it *in the present*. Ideology, however, is still lying in wait there too. For my part, I find it under many entirely idealistic ecclesiological discourses, pastoral proposals that are neither incarnated nor incarnatable, and spiritualities that have every merit except that of helping one to live history. This third ideology nourishes claims that are as frustrating as impossible: it suggests that *the present is capable of furnishing a perfectly adequate expression of the communion of faith*.

Here one finds again, in fact, the human thirst for *immediacy*, that thirst which maintains what I shall call "thaumaturgical" understandings of life. In politics, for example, can one be a party militant without considering the party the absolute remedy that will heal all immediately and forever? How can one practice

146

THE CHURCH

a new science (as has been the case with psychology and, more recently, biology) without making of it a panacea? Or speaking more experientially, how is one to "fall in love" and not believe that this "fall" is in itself the guarantee of an eternity of love? The cold wisdom of our world, whose objectivity is sometimes lauded, does not cease to revive the marvelous and the miraculous. But is not seeing the church (or inviting others to do so) as an immediate revelation of the communion of salvation subject to the same phantoms? Are intimacy with God and human solidarity self-evident? Can there be a communion, a family of God, on this side of our differences without silencing them authoritatively?

This illusion is perpetuated on one condition: on the condition of fleeing true history in order to enclose oneself in the security of a closed space where limits and egoism would be absent and would cease to remind us that it is difficult to live. This third rejection of ideology thus reveals that something very fundamental is at stake, perhaps the only question that is truly important, the question of death. By succumbing to the appetite for immediacy, the third form of idealism ushers one into a universe that calms at least momentarily our fear of living, that fear that is also and indissolubly a fear of dying. Differences and plurality promise the church a certain death, since they forbid one to confuse communion and uniformity. Can communion ever be stifled in the corset of *one* particular form, of *one* theology, for example, or *one* pastoral initiative, or *one* moral discourse? Because of the marriage in Jesus Christ of God and history, where else is one to seek ecclesiastical communion than in life as lived, which seems to scatter the church in a thousand directions in which persons and communities simultaneously translate and betray the church they believe?

"When the heart is ill at ease, we sustain it with rites," Confucius said.[7] We sustain our sick hearts with a mass that has become a thing, as the preceding chapter tried to say, or, more generally, with anemic sacraments reduced to a rituality that no

147

A CHURCH OF THE BAPTIZED

longer has anything to do with life. In fact, it would be necessary to go back up the entire chain of elements to see how the habits of each one, fascinated by the immediate, intend to elude death: through the magic of the sacraments, of course, but also through a vision of priests that permits God in the end to claim to be in human beings; through a christology for which salvation reaches us as surely as water passes through the pipe, passes from the reservoir to the faucet; and finally through God the thaumaturge who directly intervenes in history without our freedom being in any way part of his intervention.

In short, having reached this point of its journey, our reflection realizes how all ideological conceptions of communion, the third as well as the first two, reject a single challenge: that of seeking communion *in the historical mediations* that we give to it and in the places we make it exist, or, more concretely still, in the communities we build, poor and limited, and always tempted to sin by standardization. Nowhere else—neither after the time of history, nor before today, nor above the present that our communities give to communion.

2. To the Clerics Ecclesiastical Unity, to the Laity Plurality

Why have we carried out these three attacks both on the side of uniformity and on the side of communion? For a reason that I think is literally vital, i.e. of the order of life. All these ideologies finally end in the same result since each one *condemns* the concrete unity of the church to a *static condition*. They promise peace and security, but it is the peace of the tomb, a peace that is the very opposite of that promised in Jesus Christ, that sword which comes to separate the mother from her son and the brother from his sister. "Do not believe that I have come to bring peace on the earth. . . ." Uniformity and the spontaneous ways of considering communion forbid a true *passage* of the church. But

148

does not the level of questioning to which the critique has led permit us to conclude that the passage is *essential* to the church, that it is of its *nature* so that *the church simply does not exist when it is not effecting a passage?* One says the same thing again by affirming that *the unity* of the church is essentially the *genesis of unity.* Communion exists where believers translate it into communication and a "building of community."

But why, in the last analysis, does a static condition afflict our understandings of ecclesiastical unity? Why has movement ceased to define the type of cohesion that should be proper to a church that claims to go back to Easter and presents itself as the sacrament of this same Easter? I have tried to show how none of the ideologies considered is capable of integrating *plurality* in its understanding of ecclesiastical unity. For my part, I am convinced that this integration remains even today the major challenge that life and ecclesiology have to face.

Do all these considerations help us to take a new look at the present structure of clergy/laity relations? Such is the aim we now have to pursue.

I shall first of all note a curious phenomenon. Reflecting on what is happening in the present discourses of the hierarchy, the *Lineamenta* have partially cleaned up the customary vocabulary since there is never any mention there of "clerics" or of "clergy," except for a short passage that speaks as vaguely as it does rapidly of possible "attempts at a '*clericalization of the laity*' or of a '*laicization of the clergy*' pointed out by Pope John Paul II."[8] On the other hand, the terms "lay people" and "laity" are abundantly used from one end to the other. In my opinion, that reveals a twofold disrespect for concrete ecclesiastical life. On the one hand, one thus lets it be understood that the priests, the bishops, and the pope have finally ceased thinking of themselves as clerics and speaking and behaving like clerics. The least one can say is that such a judgment is a purely intellectual view. On the other hand, the authors of the *Lineamenta* give the impression that the

149

A CHURCH OF THE BAPTIZED

laity can be defined otherwise than in its relations with the clergy, and I am quite afraid that they are then speaking of everything except the church as it is still experienced today. But it is necessary to take a closer look.

The Clergy as the Sacrament of Ecclesiastical Unity

Still situating itself at the top in the life of the church, or pushed by lay people themselves to consider themselves as the sole subject of ecclesiastical unity, the clergy continues to favor the loss of the church in ideology in two ways.

1. It is a truism to say that the clergy has sinned by a *standardization* of life. One can see day after day that it still does not bear differences well and that it favors relationships that leave no place to the uniqueness of persons and communities. It has quite evidently blocked the movements of the church. Is it inviting the church today to live the passages that its situation in history demands? One often speaks of the inevitable delay of the church with respect to the march of human history, affirming (which is surely not totally false) that a healthy wisdom and its long experience keep it from bowing to fashions that, when all is said and done, are ephemeral. But when wisdom takes such a long time, sometimes centuries, to adjust ecclesiastical structures, one begins to suspect that there is more to it than wisdom or concern for faithfulness to the gospel.

A few illustrations in the form of questions will suffice to show how the privileged place of the clergy has paralyzed and still concretely paralyzes the passages that the church, at the invitation of history, should nevertheless effect. Why has it taken so long for Catholic thought to deliver itself from Thomism, and from a Thomism that, for all that, is rather foreign to the bubbling dynamism of St. Thomas? Theology has lost a considerable amount of time with respect to the new languages in which humanity is trying to express itself, and we are still exhausting ourselves wanting to make up for lost time. Along the same lines,

150

what efforts and generosity have to be summoned today in order to do justice to the tasks defined at the beginning of the century by modernism, tasks that Pius X could not (or would not) "regulate" otherwise than by imposing the anti-modernist oath on theologians? Furthermore, how long will a parish be maintained as the only generally recognized ecclesiastical structure that quite evidently, and because of its claims to exclusivity, favors anonymity and uniformity and no longer suffices to nourish the communal desires of believers? The churches of the third world are teaching us that something else is possible; but one knows the price they have to pay to demonstrate it to us and that the drop in the numbers of the clergy is surely not indifferent to the delays recorded elsewhere. Another illustration: Will the present organization of immense dioceses be indefinitely conserved with a bishop at their head whom persons and communities see on a purely occasional basis when problems force them to go to meet him or (often out of pastoral "duty") he accords them the privilege of a visit? Are "simple priests" still going to consent for a long time to being consulted on the choice of their bishop by a process whose normal outcome has it that in the end this choice totally escapes them? And how much longer will the bishops and episcopal conferences accept relations with the pope and his curia where they always come out the losers as soon as what is at stake has some relevance and uniformity is threatened? What beats all perhaps is when it is a priori forbidden that a question be posed, for example, that about the ecclesiastical discipline of mandatory "priestly celibacy"—as if a question could be prevented from being a question, and as if the best response were to refuse to listen to the question! There is no point in insisting further. So much proof has been given so consistently that clerics empty life as long as they situate themselves at the top in the church in order to standardize it or as long as, within the clergy itself, the highest clerics organize themselves to control those on the bottom.

    2. I do not want to leave this field of the structural situation

A CHURCH OF THE BAPTIZED

of the clergy without saying a word about my greatest current fear. Today an invitation is issued to all to forsake clericalism in order to bring a church of communion into existence. Priests, bishops, and pope are often the first to formulate this wish. But, as I have tried to say, the communion presented is often a dream, an alienating dream, since it is unrelated to the actual state of the church and the present moment of its history. One of the perversities of this bad abstraction is that it leaves the field entirely open for controls as totalitarian as those that are in play in the imposition of uniformity. And my fear is seeing these discourses on communion put lay people and communities to sleep while the clerics continue their concrete controls. The latter have, in effect, begun to learn, especially since Vatican II, to forsake the narrow domain of the mass and of the sacramental system in order to think now of their ecclesiastical place in terms of *unity*. I shall say further on to what extent this orientation seems to me entirely legitimate. But the little that I have advanced about the concrete cohesion of the church will suffice (at least I hope so) to make it understood that ecclesiastical unity is a *complex* reality: this unity is indissolubly *communion* and *plurality*. Here is the danger and the reason for my fears: *because of the complexity of the historical unity of the church, and in virtue of our long background of clericalism, some are already handing plurality over to the lay persons, whereas they reserve the right and the privilege of sacramentalizing communion for the clerics.*

That is why I so fear theological statements like the following: "In relation to the church where he has been chosen, the priest will in one sense appear as the sacrament of the priesthood of the faithful."[9] But why would the faithful be powerless to sacramentalize their own priesthood themselves? If others are trusted with doing so in their place, it is because they have been afflicted with some infirmity. Speaking more directly along the lines of the preceding developments, I have read in several theolo-

152

THE CHURCH

gies of the ordained ministry that priests and bishops are the sacrament of the unity of the church. Could the communities thus not be the sacrament of the unity of the church that they are? These approaches are intolerable from a Christian point of view. In effect, they make us fall again into the dichotomy that the preceding chapters analyzed by separating communion in order to entrust it to the guardianship of the priests, the bishops, and the pope. Are we condemned always to repeat the same errors? Are we going to put the new wine of Vatican II into the old wineskins of our customary structures?

To Lay People the Plurality

The world of temporal affairs is entrusted to lay people as proper to them.[10] *Evangelii nuntiandi*, an apostolic exhortation of Paul VI, specifies the tasks that fall to lay people in this way: "Their own field of evangelizing activity is the vast and complicated world of politics, society and economics, but also the world of culture, of the sciences and the arts, of international life, of the mass media. It also includes other realities which are open to evangelization, such as human love, the family, the education of children and adolescents, professional work, suffering."[11] This is indeed a vast and complicated world. One could add that the clerics are very fortunate to escape it! But I fear above all the price (and I mean the properly *ecclesiastical* price) that the present structures of the church make lay people pay. Is this whole world not entrusted to them so that, during this time, the internal life of the church can remain under the thumb of the clerics?

In effect, all the domains mentioned by Paul VI need a type of intervention that runs counter precisely to uniformity as well as to ideological reductions of communion. And that is for a very simple reason in the end: *all these domains are the place where plurality ineluctably arises.* Except for situations of flagrant injustice, is there ever "one" political choice that imposes itself as

153

being "the" Christian choice, a choice thoroughly in accord with faith? And, further, who could say whether capitalism *or* socialism is the option to be chosen in the present organization of the world economy? Do not all the societies that comprise minorities (is there a single one, for that matter, that does not?) show that cultural unanimity is possible only where a majority stifles the minorities? Plurality puts its seal on short-term relations as well: just think of the multiple faces of love, of the differences in mentality that render so difficult the task of parents in educating their children, of solitude in suffering, a solitude that often threatens to turn into isolation, so much is it an entirely original and difficult communicable experience. The world (which, once again, defines the specific nature of the laity) makes the church to be written in the plural. But are we, clerics in particular, really ready to write ecclesiastical *unity* in the plural?

From its first part, the text of the *Lineamenta* speaks of two "tendencies that pose problems," two tendencies that, "within the framework of the vocation and the specifically secular mission of lay people," "incur certain critiques." I shall cite the passage that deals with the first tendency.

> *The first tendency concerns those lay people who are involved with temporal and earthly affairs. They are so influenced by secularization as to refuse, or at least compromise, that fundamental and unrenounceable link with the faith, which alone is capable of generating and supporting that "Christian animation" which must make alive the activity of the laity in the temporal order.*

> *There is no scarcity of forms of collaboration in the economic, social, political and cultural areas in which the Christian laity renounce their "identity" by adopting criteria and methods which the faith does not share:*

THE CHURCH

> *in these and similar cases "secularity" becomes "secular-*
> *ism," which is a radical contradiction of the true secular*
> *vocation of the Christian laity.*[12]

The *Lineamenta* criticize here the loss of faith within the limits of a temporal commitment, and I do too! But because the limits of the temporal (entrusted to lay people as proper to them) always betray the unlimited character of faith, can lay people be anything other than "collaborators" in always doubtful intentions and incapable of resisting "secularism"? That was shown above. The little that I said about ecclesiastical unity, however, permits us to take up the set of problems developed there at another level. Since they are sent into the world as the place of their ecclesiastical responsibility, and because this world is inevitably manifold, are not lay people condemned always to pervert the Christian "identity" and always to rupture the unity of the church?

There is indeed "the fundamental and absolute relation to the *faith*," where this faith defines the Christian identity. But this statement only postpones the problem further and reveals what is truly at stake. *Who will say what the faith is? Who will define what believing means?* Surely not lay people whose proper domain is precisely that which seems to scatter the faith in all directions. Always at the bottom, like the victims of an evil fate, lay people are not a defining subject of the faith (and I mean concretely in the life of the church today and in spite of contrary affirmations about the *sensus fidelium*, for example). They continue to receive passively the definitions that are elaborated elsewhere, an identity card where it is difficult to see who could confer it if not the priests, the bishops, and the pope.

I spoke of a price that lay people must pay when one speaks of their specific nature in terms of the world. I shall return to this point in the next chapter. But the result of this process can already be seen: the more one entrusts the world to lay people,

155

A CHURCH OF THE BAPTIZED

the more the church can rest under the control of the clergy during this time.

3. "You Are the Church!"

A short while ago, John Paul II cried out these enthusiastic and exciting words to several thousand young people: "You are the church!"[13] This cry no doubt sprang from a sincere desire to restore to all a church that should never have ceased belonging to them. Furthermore, this desire is shared to a large extent today by bishops and priests and, above all, by many lay people who continue to keep the church close to their hearts. Why, then, are there such difficulties? Why do we withdraw from lay people what has just been entrusted to them as soon as they begin to do justice to this freshly acquired dignity and responsibility? No doubt, a number of reasons are operative, but one will understand that there is one to which I, for my part, attach greater importance: neither the clergy nor the laity can realize their desire without coming up against a structure of relationships of which we are all the heirs and which often offers fierce resistance even in those who wish for something else.

Let us not deceive ourselves: we are all indeed called to an ecclesiastical and an ecclesiological conversion. In the last part of this chapter, which is already too long and nevertheless too short, four points will show somewhat the measure of this conversion. For each point, I shall first indicate what is at stake globally, then what it implies on the part of lay people and on the part of ordained ministers (priests, bishops, and pope), and finally what it demands as a transformation of the present relationships between clergy and laity.

For a Church Becoming Church

The critique of ideology will at least have shown to what extent we spontaneously see the church as a static reality that

156

THE CHURCH

never changes, cannot change, or takes an interminable time to adapt. For my part, I believe that the church takes on meaning only in those for whom *being church is becoming church.* That is particularly true concerning the *unity* of the church, and it is at this level that I should like to take up the problem again.

As one rich in a competence acquired over a long period of time, Yves Congar writes: "Recent centuries have bequeathed us an *objectivist* and *fixated* conception of unity. The one writing these lines has been penetrated by it to such a point that it is difficult for him to envisage anything else. But it is necessary to do so. We saw unity as an existing framework with defined limits and rules in which it was necessary to remain, or to which it was necessary to return, if one had left it, and to adhere by conforming to its norms. The role of authority was to specify these norms and to watch over their observance."[14] We thus find again, this time with respect to ecclesiastical unity, the objectivism and the reification of the preceding chapters. I was perhaps not mistaken in affirming the extreme coherence of our general religious mentality. What is now brought out with greater clarity is the *fixation* that has so burdened our concrete life and our mental schemas. I have tried to say to what extent this fixation prevents in more precise terms the progress of ecclesiastical unity through standardization or through enclosing communion in an ideological apparatus unrelated to life. If this is indeed what "recent centuries have bequeathed us," a few years will certainly not suffice to convert our habitual ways of speaking and doing. But this is indeed the challenge: *to pass from a static cohesion based on the tranquil feeling of a possession of the truth to a communion given in such a way that the unity of the church is always before us.*

What does this challenge imply on the part of lay people? To take up the words of Congar again, they have been accustomed to consider the church "as a pre-existing framework," a unity so tightly woven that their sole responsibility was one of "conformity" "to the norms" specified by others. That is very precisely

157

A CHURCH OF THE BAPTIZED

what defined and still defines their status as lay people. There is an "inside" defined in minute detail and thus an equally evident "outside," which has the particular advantage of permitting "the authority" to excommunicate quite expeditiously. Appealing now to a church of which they are the subject, lay people must learn (and some are discovering it already) that the church only exists where all, favored with a communion that debars none, are in the process of *making community*, of *building community*.

From this perspective, is not the only possible excommunication that which recognizes that a person or a community which has ceased *to become* church has excluded itself from ecclesiastical unity? That strangely shifts our customary way of posing many questions. In particular, the ministerial service of the priests, the bishops, and the pope seems illuminated in a new way. They are not the absolute and tyrannical masters of the norms, no more than they are responsible for their application or judges of an orthodoxy that they have defined a priori themselves. They are there *to serve the ecclesiastical genesis of persons and communities*.

From this point of view, it will one day be necessary to restore its entire importance to a little text of *The Ministry and Life of Priests* that expresses the end of ordained ministry, a text very few theologians (in fact, none that I know) bother to comment on. When the decree places priests and bishops in the wake of the historical Jesus in section two, it says that their ministry is necessary for a single solitary reason: "*ut (fideles) in unum coalescerent corpus*," in order that the faithful may grow and increase in the unity of a single body. For me, that is how the most promising lines are drawn for the future of both the ministers and the theology of the ordained ministry. Among all the points that I should like to raise here, two are of more immediate interest for the new relationships that the clergy is invited to live with the church. On the one hand, this text lets the end of ordained ministry breathe again insofar as priests, bishops, and pope do not receive a "power over the mass" but, more generally, are ordained

158

THE CHURCH

to serve the *unity* of the church, the communal growth of all. These are the persons and communities, moreover, that are the subject of the verb *"coalescerent"* ("in order that all may grow and increase"); these are thus the subject responsible for their own growth. Far from being the first and the last guarantor of it, all the ministers (from the "simple priest" to the pope) are its good servants if they *constantly decenter themselves in favor of this growth for which all bear the responsibility.*

Is there not in such a short sentence something that would revolutionize the usual relations between clerics and lay people? As the guardian of a standardizing orthodoxy, the clergy assures its domination over lay people by the absolutization, the "canonization" one could say, of its own condition as the subject of ecclesiastical unity. A radically new relationship is put forth (it is already being lived where lay people have forsaken the laity) as soon as the condition of subject is restored to all. All, in effect, are learning to appropriate for themselves three statements that the clergy had drawn to its side: we *are* church; we are *responsible* for the church and its unity; this being as well as this responsibility is lived nowhere else than in our *human decisions*, both personal and collective. This is what the three following points wish to render explicit.

"In Him, All Christians Become a Holy and Royal Priesthood"

In our super-consumption societies where the utilitarian prevails, where so many artificial needs are created that they end by extinguishing desire, we have learned to manufacture things according to *lacks*. Does the same hold for the church? Is it a genesis of unity with the sole end of filling a void because it has a need to gather everything in by spreading everywhere at all times? Are Christians building community because of an absence, to fill a void, and finally to consume what is lacking to them? Faithful to what was said above about the christological foundations of the church, I submit the following statement: it is rather *in virtue of a*

159

A CHURCH OF THE BAPTIZED

surplus that all together build community. Communion, in effect, is too much a part of them for them ever to be satisfied with isolation or with the present state of their communal life. They are working to grow and to increase in the unity of a single body by the grace of a communion that is always already there, faithfully assured because it has been accomplished in the passover of Jesus Christ. Is that alienation?

Realism, in effect, notices the immense danger that those who invite lay people to take charge of the church make them incur. Certain lay people perceive this danger and resist or reject it. But many others, often naively, hardly suspect that they are heading toward a still omnipresent clericalism. How many persons and communities have burned their wings there! Discouragement and abdication lie in wait, without mentioning everything that makes one confuse revolt and revolution. What will give them the courage to remain alive for long, ecclesiastically alive? In the last analysis, once the political practices have been explained in detail that help one to live while waiting for something else to be instituted (which I do not have the leisure to make explicit here), I see only one motivation that is sufficient to nourish commitment and perseverance in commitment: the certitude *of faith* that a communion precedes us all which we *hope* will always be stronger than the innumerable obstacles that try to kill it. "For in him all the faithful are made a holy and royal priesthood" (MLP, no. 2). This text does not conjugate communion in the future; it confesses it as a present reality: in the passover of Jesus Christ "all" become "one." Are we really Christian believers if we do not believe that? The realism of faith perhaps does not resemble the realisms that have been defined for us. But is that not precisely the reason that it promises a true revolution? In a word, individuals and groups will not be community, or will quickly cease wishing to become such, without the certitude that *they are such*. There is no true subject that does not have to *become* what he or she already *is*.

160

THE CHURCH

It would be necessary to reflect a long time on this last proposition. I must content myself with suggesting the capital importance that it assumes for a new understanding of the ordained ministry. The presence of communion in every person and community that confesses Jesus Christ as Lord, a communion that wishes to dwell in them as a surplus, makes ordained ministers unable to behave in just any way in their relations to the laity. If the confession is true, the pope, the bishops, and the priests will approach persons and communities *with the certitude of going to meet a communion that is already there.* They do not bring Jesus Christ, they do not come to give him; they are thus not the reified mediators of a communion that, without them, would have forsaken the church. They set out to meet a communion that awaits them in the life of each and all. They are going to serve the historical growth of what is freely offered, offered with none debarred. This perspective, which has hardly been opened here, implies many transformations in both our theologies of the ordained ministry and the concrete way in which ministers are invited to manage their lives. Is a criterion not found there, to give just one illustration, that is quite fundamental in the choice of priests, bishops, and pope? In effect, how could one be ordained who only knows how to "give"? The criterion would thus be the following: no one can be ordained who is not sufficiently *available* always to welcome and to favor the growth of a communion that precedes him *in the life* of the persons and communities that he agrees to serve.

At bottom, the entire ecclesiastical structure is invited here to conversion. Because it continues today to favor the passivity of lay persons, how could it help them to nourish their pride in the surplus that dwells in them and that they themselves are? This pride must be learned, it seems to me, as well as this awareness of a surplus. Everything in ecclesiastical life should become a pedagogical place in the service of this awareness without which ecclesiastical life withers and dies. This holds for absolutely every-

161

thing, including the sacraments. It also includes the ordained ministry: persons and communities are favored with a communion which no one can take from them. They are the ones who are through and through the true subject of the church.

The Unity of the Church: A Unity of Plurality

Christian realism forbids one ever to cease confessing the surplus of salvation. That is the sin of uniformity. It is also the sin that all the initiatives still commit today that wish to impose by force "one" way of thinking, of speaking, and of doing, even and especially if to justify this totalitarianism one claims to be the guardian of ecclesiastical communion. It is there that the sin against the Spirit is found (which is no doubt the only true sin) and not on the side of commitments that make Christian communion exist historically. In effect, Christian realism designates history as the sole habitat of the church and its communion. How, then, could ecclesiastical unity not encounter differences and plurality there? Hence the urgency of another conversion: *ecclesiastical unity must become a unity in plurality.*

Constrained to uniformity or fooled by dreams of communion without any relation to the march of history, believers have forgotten in the course of centuries the meaning of the other *as other.* Of course, they have had to experience this difference, for it arises as soon as one forsakes the position of a spectator to become an artisan of history. What I mean is that plurality was not integrated ecclesiastically and that it is not always valued in the church of today or in the majority of our theologies of the church.[15] Should one be surprised by the fact that personally and communally we have so much trouble conjugating ecclesiastical unity in the plural? But the relationships of Jesus Christ with history (if it is indeed to him that we appeal) urge all believers to learn the ecclesiastical meaning of their irreducible differences by letting them emerge, by permitting them to be expressed, but also by deciding to locate the church's work of communion there.

THE CHURCH

This is such an immense challenge that there are days when one may think oneself incapable of accepting it. Persons and communities then realize, in effect, how the unity of the church is not built up in history without inevitable tensions that often lie at the heart of conflicts that make division and dispersion, far from being a theoretical danger, concretely threaten the cohesion of the church.

How can lay persons be invited to convert their relationships to ecclesiastical unity without issuing an invitation to the priests, the bishops, and even the pope? Having learned for a long time that they are the possessors of unity, and pushing their pride to the point of taking possession of it by standardizing the churches and the church, it is easy for clerics to impose their authority on lay people: they will say, for example, that the latter will tear one another to pieces as soon as one ceases to dictate to them "the" correct way of thinking and acting. But as soon as they standardize the ordained ministers are themselves perverted. They lose the meaning of their service, at least in the sense that Vatican II affirmed it. The council does not charge them with substituting a static condition for life nor, what comes to the same thing, uniformity for a unity of plurality. It rather consecrates them to serve growth and the progress of all toward the *unity* of the body of Christ.[16] This building up of the church is simply not possible as long as each person and community does not make an original contribution to it. Even if that seems paradoxical or contradictory to them in view of what they have learned for a long time, ordained ministers are good servants of the church when they serve the emergence of originality and an ecclesiastical encounter of differences.

To be a believing Christian is to consent to the constant invitation that Jesus Christ issues to convert oneself to history and its laws. And that is why being church is making church, why living communion is entering into communication and building community. It is useless to seek the church elsewhere. It exists

163

A CHURCH OF THE BAPTIZED

only where persons and communities, urged on by communion, set out again and again to encounter one another. If such is indeed the case, clergy/laity relationships can no longer be from subject to object, and that is why the only future of their present organization is the disappearance of this organization. Who could substitute for any given individual in this work and this genesis without blocking the work and the genesis as a result and thus killing the church as the sacrament of Jesus Christ? In all persons and communities there is realized such a loving encounter with communion and plurality that all are *the* subject of the church.

Deciding To Make Church

History shows us that the church has never been a self-evident reality. We see that it is not self-evident today either and suspect that this will always be the case. If its unity is communion and plurality, these two poles being necessary to understand it and to live it well, the marriage between communion and plurality will never be consummated in a magical manner independently of human freedom. Another conversion is thus suggested, the most fundamental one perhaps, which forsakes the perverse abstraction of uniformity and an alienating understanding of communion in order to situate ecclesiastical unity *in the human decision* of believers. In short, *the church simply does not exist when persons and communities do not decide to make it exist.*

Certain reductionist oversimplifications translate the fidelity of Jesus Christ into a sort of automatic permanence, as if the church could last without our having to recreate it unceasingly. The most deceptive of these oversimplifications is that which has recourse to the New Testament itself in order to justify the abdication to which (unconsciously, I hope) it invites us: it is then stated that the church in any case "has the promise of eternal life." How can anyone be so blind and not recognize the facts? For it is a fact that the church has simply disappeared from

164

THE CHURCH

regions (and even from the larger part of continents) where it had once flourished. Nothing guarantees that this will not be the case in the future; many indices even show that it is already experiencing important losses here and there. By discovering that they are subjects of the church, lay people are learning (they are no doubt called to learn it more and more) that ecclesiastical communion does not work without them, that they have to decide again and again in favor of it. More concretely, that means that the wager of the community demands an unceasing investment of their responsible freedom. No community serves the Christian encounter of persons without the latter having to *decide* to make community. Communities cease to be church the moment, yielding to the illusory charms of a tranquil possession of the truth, each one no longer decides to approach the others. Ecclesiastical community thus exists only where persons and communities *decide* to translate it into *communication* between persons and communities.

When clerics standardize life, they are serving the exact opposite of this dynamic. Why would the "simple faithful" seek one another out if certain ones already held the answer and knew the secret of unity? What would remain to impel communities to encounter differences, to communicate with other communities, when, thanks to the priest or the bishop, each one is already certain that "elsewhere" will be identical to "here"? Turning now to the service of the pope, one can ask if he is faithful to his service when he appeals to the past or to a privilege that he alone enjoys in appealing to the past in order to define the present and thus to take away from the churches the responsibility of deciding today what tomorrow will be made of?

In one sense, the more priests and bishops truly live their service, the less persons and communities will be led to resort to them to decide in their place. This is already noticeable where Christians are inventing a new way of being church: they can no longer tolerate the totalitarianism of clerics and prefer to assume the risk of their decisions. They often hesitate, seek, doubt, and

165

A CHURCH OF THE BAPTIZED

err. And they sometimes find at least enough to decide to continue. Is it not this stubbornness which constantly remakes community that gives wings to Christian hope? At that moment the confession has ceased to be a proclamation unrelated to history because the church has finally found its true subject again.

7

The World

To Lay People the World of Temporal Realities

We have now reached the last element of the schema: thanks to the *priests*, the *mass* completes a *church* that can then go out to the *world*. Situated at the bottom, entirely at the bottom, the world is evidently not included in any way at all. On the basis of the preceding chapters, one can already presume that it is the term of a long deductive movement, an exclusively deductive movement, that has unfolded from the beginning. As God was *the subject*, an absolute beginning and an absolute of beginning, so the world risks being commonly perceived as the radical *object*, a passive thing in total dependence, that has to receive everything from above, from the elements above.

But this presumption does not suffice. It is necessary to verify the validity of what can already be guessed. In the dynamics of clergy/laity relations, the world is operative as too decisive an element for it to be neglected. It is said that the world is the proper domain of lay people, that which specifies their place in the logic of traditional ecclesiology and in the concrete structure of the church today. It thus constitutes a necessary detour for anyone who desires to clarify the ecclesiastical situation of the laity.

I am anxious, however, to repeat that the objective is not and cannot be the elaboration of a Christian theology of the world. I simply wish to look at the *relations* that Christians have learned to live with what is commonly called "the world."[1] It is in the relations themselves that everything is decided; it is thus these relations that will determine the possible place or non-place of lay people in the church.

A CHURCH OF THE BAPTIZED

Two other clarifications are necessary. Because the world is *the absolute bottom*, I shall not take up each of the preceding elements again but shall speak more globally of the *top* even though it may mean giving greater importance from time to time, for the purpose of illustration, to one or the other of the elements situated above the world. I should also point out that, contrary to the structure of the preceding chapters, there will not be a moment explicitly devoted to clergy/laity relations. The set of themes relating to the world is too important not to try to specify as we proceed the fate that is reserved for these relations and thus the real ecclesiastical weight of the clergy and the laity.

1. The World in the Contemporary Religious Mentality

Section no. 31 of *Lumen Gentium* entrusts to lay people "the activation of all Christian and gospel virtualities which are certainly hidden but already present and active in the realities of the world." It is nevertheless clear that, when Christians today speak of the world and their relations to it, they do not begin at zero and cannot appeal to a sort of virginity that would be the virginity of the beginnings of the world. The past has taught them things about it, a mentality has developed, they are heirs of a certain vision and of a certain type of behavior. The risk I wish to run is naming this still present heritage. From the *anonymity* of the world to the perception of it as an *occasion of guilt*, such are the two terms, apparently unrelated but intimately connected by a certain logic, of a movement of which I shall single out five moments.

When the World Is So Much Everything That It Is No Longer Anything

The notion of the world is bathed in conceptual haziness. Some will believe that this is a question for intellectuals without importance for "real life." But this haziness is always dangerous

168

THE WORLD

in that it favors a soft life and the weakness of commitments. Does not the restoration of the world into the hands of lay people have as an inevitable consequence with respect to ecclesiastical organization the loss of the identity of the laity in precisely this haziness, in a generality without content? I submit, in effect, the following hypothesis: *the specific nature of the clergy appears all the more evident as that of the laity continues to swim in imprecision*. This first trait, in fact, takes up again a little principle that is as important as it is simple: when everything is everything in history, everything ends by no longer being anything. *Everything* is entrusted to lay people when the world is entrusted to them. But is this not the reason that they end by no longer being anything ecclesiastically?

1. I shall first take up *Evangelii nuntiandi*, the exhortation of Paul VI already cited above, contenting myself with the enumeration of what this text has the generosity of entrusting to lay people.[2] In the domain of short-term relations, of what forms the tissue of the close relationships that one has to live with oneself and with others, there fall to lay people *love*, the *family*, the *education of children and of adolescents*, one's *professional work*, and *suffering*. Is anything lacking there that makes the life of a man or a woman in the universe of his or her short-term relations to be simply a human life? To this there is added the vast domain of long-term relations. This time, the specific nature of the laity will find itself living in *politics*, the *social realm*, the *economy* and *culture*, the *sciences* and the *arts*, *international life*, and finally the *mass media*. Such is the "vast and complicated world" that is entrusted to lay people. Such are the horizons toward which they are sent and which, in principle, define them as lay people.

History shows that the clerics can become involved in almost all these sectors: some were great artists, others pursued or pursue a scientific career, others still work today in the mass media. There are, however, two exceptions. The sad history of worker priests (especially in France) and other more recent exam-

169

A CHURCH OF THE BAPTIZED

ples show clearly enough that clerics cannot "be involved in politics." Furthermore, priests and bishops are obliged to renounce two aspects of love: conjugal love and parental love. *Politics* and *marriage* thus constitute two domains where prohibitions are operative. It will be necessary to recall this as the analysis continues.

With respect to lay people, the theory would have it that practically nothing of what makes history escapes them. This is what seems to confer a remarkable nobility and extension to their lives and their commitments. In one sense, is this not a bit too much? A friend told me (fortunately with a lot of humor) the really unbelievable extent of his ecclesiastical commitment. Though married, the father of five children, and involved in diverse sectors of collective life, he was further responsible for the diocesan office for "lay ministry." But the ridiculousness of this responsibility began to manifest itself the day he realized that he was living with a laywoman, bringing up five little lay people, playing sports with lay people, pursuing his socio-political commitments with lay people, in short, living in constant contact with lay people of all conditions. Did he have by mandate pastoral responsibility for this whole world? Was he sent to *everyone* in *every* life situation proper to each one? If the world defines the specific nature of the laity, does lay ministry not become responsible for *everything*, so much so that it no longer has anything as a particular ecclesiastical end?

2. In effect, *the world is* still today *ecclesiastically nothing.* That is why *lay people*, defined by this world, *have no real weight in the organization of ecclesiastical life.* Such is the question that my friend was obliged by his commitments to pose to all those responsible for diocesan ministry. In virtue of what could he, to whom *everything* was entrusted, choose, decide, or prefer to go "pastorally" here rather than there? But, further, what remained for the other diocesan offices, since offices for the "liturgy," for "family life," for the "missions," etc. were also maintained? *Con-*

170

cretely speaking, these are the offices that held the power of decision concerning the place of lay people in the liturgy, family life, etc. The true ecclesiastical power concerning the laity is decided there and thus escapes the office for "lay ministry." The competent authorities finally made the only decision that was logical and sensible: the office for lay ministry was abolished.

3. This experience illustrates a much broader ecclesiastical datum: on the level of organization where the true decisions are made, our ecclesiology entrusts lay people too much with *everything* for them to be a true agent of the church.[3] And why does this generosity render lay people so powerless? In my opinion, it is for the following reason: *the world is not really a part of our understanding of the church.*

It would be enlightening to do the eventful history of ecclesiology here and to show how still today the world is not well integrated into our understandings of the church. I shall content myself with telling what, in my short life, I have personally experienced and continue to observe. There was a time, one not too distant and still present, when church/world relations were thought of in the mode of *antagonism*, one pole being opposed to the other by nature, one even having to combat the other. Such a relationship has left a deep mark on the spirituality offered during my novitiate and my seminary training, and I am (almost) certain that all adults today, in one form or another, were familiar with that type of relationship in which the church had to "fight against" the world. Then there was what I shall call the phase of *peaceful coexistence*, the church and the world constituting two poles of which each was to respect the autonomy of the other. A good illustration of this on a more theoretical level would be the long and patient work carried out in the United States in particular that the church and state might be separated, the latter having to be respected for what it is without the church dictating its truth to it. With the help of the council and above all the work of the decades that preceded it, one began to speak of *dialogue*, the

A CHURCH OF THE BAPTIZED

church and the world having no doubt interesting and important things to say to one another. It was then theoretically admitted that the church is *in* the world, that it even has an interest in "reading the signs of the times" if it wants to make sense and to be relevant.[4] But I am afraid that we are still there. How many admit *the presence of the world in the church* as a fact and assume it in their reflection? Is not this refusal to take the world into consideration, this general hesitation to situate it *in* the church, not the true cause of most of the ills from which the church is presently suffering?[5]

In particular, lay people are as absent from the places where their ecclesiastical fate is nevertheless decided as the world remains outside the church. In all the decision-making authorities, even those that deal with them and their lives, are they anything other than vague observers, "resource persons" at the most, without any real power of decision?[6] Others speak and write in their place. At the most, they may perhaps speak. Perhaps they will even be permitted to contribute to the writing. But that is precisely the question. With respect to the laity, everything that is given to lay persons is still done in the church of today by way of permission or concession. One unfortunately has to foresee that it will be that way for a long time to come.

In one sense, I hope that I am misreading life. It appears so evident to me that the clergy has every interest in continuing to give the world to lay people. The latter seem to receive everything. But in fact, ecclesiastically speaking, they receive nothing, have nothing, and are nothing, while the clergy continues to be everything and to keep the power of controlling everything.

A World That Is Not What Is Situated Above It

The world is given to lay people as an ecclesiastical alibi: How could they be the subject of the church when what is absent from the definition of the church is entrusted to them as their

THE WORLD

proper domain?[7] But why hold the world and lay people at a distance?

The world appears quite innocent when one contents oneself with enumerating the great fields of activity that it offers from personal love to international life. But another side stands out when one realizes to what extent, for the vast majority, *it is not religiously neutral*. It is not without reason that it is often and spontaneously called *profane*. The label thus attached already describes the world: of itself, it is not of the nature of the *sacred*.[8] A trail is thus opened on which reflection has to enter.

The generality of which I was speaking seems to plunge the world into a sort of religious anonymity. The Christian mentality has nevertheless not become accustomed to considering the world as a neutral reality without importance for relationships with God. But since we have not learned to understand it *in* the life of faith, and more particularly *in* ecclesiastical life, what way is left for it to exit from anonymity? History shows it in so many ways: for all practical purposes, the world can only affirm itself by saying that it *is not* the elements that hang over it in the schema. Is the fact that the laity is still today defined only by the negative not amazing? Here one has the fundamental reason for this lack of positive content.

At the end of the course, the last element of the religious schema thus inevitably refers to the first, God. This religious universe is so coherent that a question that has arisen ever since we first asked about the images of God has surfaced again. Still being perceived as absolute transcendence, God is essentially *unlimited*, the one who knows no limits. On the other hand, Christian prejudices reduce the world: it is essentially what limits our lives, it is the place of limits, if only because it disperses humanity in time and space and makes it impossible for one to be simultaneously here *and* there, today *and* tomorrow. It is thus one and the same movement that at the same time *absolutizes* the

173

A CHURCH OF THE BAPTIZED

unlimitedness of the God we imagine *and* the limits of the world. The world is what *is not* God.

Thus posed, the problem seems exaggeratedly theoretical. It nevertheless has direct effects on the most immediate conduct of personal and collective lives. In order to illustrate the implications, I am going to resort to one of the domains where a sort of prohibition strikes the clergy, that of married life. It will be seen that the question posed is far from being unrelated to the nearest challenges of life.

No one can be celibate *and* married at the same time. Even if it is admitted that celibacy and marriage are possible modes of being present to the world, neither of these two modes *is everything*. By opting for one *or* the other, each one chooses a possibility but, as a result, creates for himself or herself a concrete impossibility. Psychology shows the difficulties that there can be in making this fundamental choice. And I am not alluding to the difficulties inherent in celibacy as celibacy or in marriage as marriage. I am speaking only of the choice *between* marriage and celibacy, for the option itself delimits and limits. A single observation suffices, moreover, to name what is at stake: Who does not know married persons who continue to act "as if" they were still celibate? Who does not know persons in a poorly assumed celibacy who try to compensate for an affective lack by demanding from their relations what marriage alone could furnish them? Every choice limits, and that is why it is often postponed such a long time.

The questions of the world thus come to life again in a way illustrated by experience with an almost maddening consistency. The world limits our choices. But how does one not *absolutize* one's own choice as if it were the only truly possible choice, the paradigm to which all should conform themselves? History thus unfolds the distressing continuity of a suspicious and condemning mentality: at certain moments, it is the "normality" of celibates that is challenged, whereas, at others, celibates judge that

174

marriage condemns one to a "less generous" life than theirs. One should not hide from the fact that suspicion and condemnation operate all the more as each of the choices is made in the name of God and in reference to God. How can one maintain this reference without making "one's" choice the choice "of God," the choice that God expects from those who truly wish to dedicate themselves to him? No one can deny that this mechanism has been operative in the church through an absolutization of the celibate life, through the erection into models of those who have chosen "the state *of perfection*," as it is called, the religious life. I am hardly caricaturizing when I say that marriage is "permitted" to persons who did not have the courage to remain celibate. Hence the delays in recognizing the immense courage of married people and that celibate clerics, for example, are far from having a monopoly on generous availability, as one is still (what an illusion that is!) generally led to believe.

Reflection could continue the analysis of this issue for a long time. But what precedes suffices, it seems to me, to single out three characteristics of the present structure of clergy/laity relations.

1. Since clerics are seen as men "of God," history has assimilated them to those who have chosen the "state of perfection." This has quite evidently been operative in the imposition of religious celibacy on priests and bishops.

2. This first point is full of disastrous implications for ecclesiastical life. Among others, clerical celibacy has also (perhaps above all) taught the immense number of married lay people to situate themselves in their relations with the clergy as persons who *are not* what celibate clerics are. This problematic can be expanded in that, because of the devaluation of lay people's way of life by an excessive valuation of the way of life of the clergy, the latter's existence has made lay people learn that they *are not* what clerics are. The difficult relations between marriage and celibacy are not, of course, the only reason that accounts for the fact that the laity *are defined by the negative*. But the illustration I have

A CHURCH OF THE BAPTIZED

chosen permits one to notice to what extent this problem does in fact arise from life and the concrete relations that structure in a particular way the relationship to the world to which clerics and lay people have become accustomed.

3. This second characteristic inevitably entails a third: in virtue of the suspicion that arises as soon as one absolutizes one possibility at the expense of other possibilities, clerics do not easily refrain even today from moralizing attitudes *about* conjugal and parental life. They do not know conjugal love and continue to believe that they are experts in this domain. They have no children but know better than anyone what is at stake in procreation and rearing.

A World That Can Only Affirm Itself by Resisting

It is thus known what the world *is not*. Nevertheless, this negative approach creates attitudes and behavior patterns and even philosophies and theologies that are very contemptuous of the world, as we are now in a better position to judge.

We have hardly learned to leave the world any other choice: *it can only affirm itself by resisting the elements above*, that which the religious mentality has spontaneously situated above it. This is the third perception into which the Christian mentality has let itself be drawn: the world is that which *resists* the church in particular, it being understood that the church is then those with whom it is identified, i.e. the clergy.

Since everything is connected, it will be understood why the laity only exits from ecclesiastical anonymity when it begins *to resist* the clergy. Do Christians know only that they are lay people? Or, if they do know it, what is the content of this term for them? They gladly claim to be "believers," "baptized persons," and "Christians." But they only realize their condition as lay people the day life puts them in relation with clerics and pushes them to resist.

In order to illustrate the dynamic that is operative here, I am

176

going to come back this time to the other domain that seems forbidden to clerics, that of *political* involvement. And I am going to take up the question again at the heart of the crisis that Catholic Action experienced, that decisive experience of the church of the twentieth century. The crisis of Catholic Action, in effect, seems to me exemplary in that it reveals a certain understanding of the church, the world, and above all relationships between the church and the world. It also illustrates the true ecclesiastical status of both lay people and clergy. For my part, I do not believe that we have finished learning the lessons that the church should have drawn from it. Four points will say well enough what is at stake.

1. Catholic Action originated from the following realization: the masses were distanced from the gospel and the pledge of liberation that Christian salvation proposes to the world. Above all, one noticed the pronounced distance of the working world that the church had lost, or, according to some, to whom the church had never been present. The church would thus *commission* lay people that they might carry the good news of salvation into the world. But because of this "commission" the members of Catholic Action found themselves quickly enough torn between two loyalties.

2. On the one hand, the pervading ecclesiology makes the church that commissions to be the hierarchy in practice. "The intention of associating the laity with the mission of the church," writes Christian Duquoc, "failed in part owing to the extremely widespread thought at that time of an *identity* between the mission of the church and the function of the hierarchy."[9] The defect, which I said above continues to defigure the Christian mentality today, thus manifests itself: the church is *identified* with the hierarchy. The church *is* the clergy. From this perspective, the members of Catholic Action become responsible for ecclesiastical unity, *but such as it is defined by the clergy:* a unity of *uni-formity.*

177

A CHURCH OF THE BAPTIZED

3. Furthermore, those commissioned want to have an effect on life, to change something in the organization of the world, for they were sent precisely to build up the world. But the more they commit themselves, the more they discover that the world, which has become their world, refuses to enter into the standardizing framework defined by the hierarchy. In particular, certain Christians are adopting more "liberal" positions; in the field of politics, for example, they are beginning to flirt with parties whose philosophies are judged unacceptable by the clergy.

4. Their fidelity to the world thus leads lay people to notice how this world resists, in politics, for example, the ecclesiastical unity that the clergy wishes to impose. But as they go along, it is lay people who *are themselves beginning to resist the clergy*. What followed and how the crisis was resolved is well known.

That is why the crisis of Catholic Action appears typical to me as well as revelatory of a still general mentality. The church will experience similar crises as long as the Christian meaning of what is called the world is not better clarified. Do certain churches, for example, wish to institute "new ministries" and "to commission" lay people for the purpose of these ministries? Because of the present structure of the church (and of the place it gives to the world), it can be foreseen that these ministries will end up in the same impasses as Catholic Action. The more lay people today try to meet the world into which the hierarchy sends them as the place of their specific ecclesiastical nature, the more this world exits from anonymity and reveals its own laws. If their religious mentality is really fashioned in the manner described in the preceding chapters, how could lay persons perceive the world otherwise than in the mode of resistance, resistance to all the elements above, including God? Hence the second question, inseparable from the first: on the level of ecclesiastical life and organization, do lay people have any other way to define their identity than that of their resistance to the clergy? For my part, I observe that this implacable law of resistance is operative every-

178

where lay people have begun and continue to assume responsibility for the church that they confess themselves to be.

The World as Obstacle

For a long time, Christians have become accustomed to living relations with the world as that "which is not at the top" and "which resists" the elements at the top, its ultimate resistance being played out vis-à-vis God. They have thus developed a fatalistic conception in which the world ends by being perceived as the *obstacle* that prevents them from elevating themselves, from leaving the bottom in order to enter into the true world. More precisely still, the *limits* of the world are considered essentially as what must be overcome at any cost in order finally to attain God, to enter truly into the life of Christ and the celebration of the mass, and to live the true church of Jesus Christ. There is absolutely no need of a long and rigorous demonstration in order to say to what extent this fourth trait of relationships with the world still leaves a deep mark on persons and communities.

It is often said in French, "Les chrétiens ont la chair triste" (literally: "Christians have sad flesh"). This judgment is no doubt justified, so much were human needs devalued, which are the lot of every existence in the world. This is true above all of the need "to love and to be loved," to use a current expression. But authoritarianism is powerless to decree the disappearance of needs; they are too much a part of us to be able to be effaced without our effacing ourselves, without absenting ourselves from our humanity. Is this not what explains the "sadness" to which allusion was made? By wishing to conquer at any price the obstacle represented by needs, one ends by stifling the humanity of persons and communities and killing a reality as important as the pleasure of living. Women are thus produced who are "obliged to perform their conjugal duty," religious for whom their communal life is no longer the fruit of desire but an occasion to fulfill otherwise frustrated needs, an understanding of fidelity for

A CHURCH OF THE BAPTIZED

which the only thing that matters is sticking it out, even if the desire is no longer there to renew the initial choice, etc. Should one be surprised if, by a return of things that is in no way mysterious, our civilization (which is nevertheless called "Christian") has begun to create artificial needs, to confuse need and desire, and to canonize the unrestrained satisfaction of desires, as if the emergence of desire were endless? Considering desire as an obstacle inevitably prepares for its absolutization.

How is this obstacle constituted by the world to be overcome? A miraculous, thaumaturgic intervention of the elements above is necessary to do so. The exclusively deductive logic thus forces each element above to maintain properly thaumaturgic relations with the limits of the world. But such relations are poorly adapted to time, to the limits of time, to its delays and its hesitations. How can one nourish a loving tenderness for human limits when the latter, in their delays and their limitations, tarry before these allegedly miraculous interventions? In the last few decades especially, political life has exhibited here a problem of relationships that is poorly resolved because it is poorly posed. Many Christians have, in effect, rediscovered the necessity of wedding faith and political commitment. All that is very legitimate, except that many immediately transferred the a-historical absolute of their visions of faith into political commitment. More precisely, their idealism and their ideologies have been directly transmuted into political commitment, the latter promising a liberation of collective relationships that is simultaneously rapid and durable, practically instantaneous and "once for all": *everything* will change, *immediately* and *for all time*. Unfortunately for these idealists, political life has its own constraining limits, its gains often taking a long time to come and never being definitively assured. Faith *and* politics were no doubt not respected for themselves in the process. The results of these disastrous telescopings can still be noticed today. Some Christians have abdicated; they have withdrawn from their territories, the territories of their

THE WORLD

"faith," forever disillusioned by the world of politics, that obstacle too stubborn for one to expend energies there that could serve so much better elsewhere. Before the resistance of the obstacles encountered, still others have concluded that faith definitely has the nature of an illusion, that it is in any case incapable of changing anything in the course of the world. In spite of these apparently divergent conclusions, it seems to me that both the ones and the others concretely affirm the world as an absolute *obstacle*.

Death constitutes the limit experience here. All sorts of voluntarist spiritualities have taught one to experience it as the ultimate obstacle, the last one to be overcome before finally reaching the other side, the side of God, which is everything and is situated at the very top. This questions in a peculiar way our alleged faith in death and resurrection as a reality already and always active in human history. The ravages of voluntarism, however, appear even more serious when it perverts the relations to all those anticipated deaths represented by sufferings and illness. It is, of course, necessary to work unceasingly to overcome suffering and illness. That is thus not the question. What angers me are all those deformations of Christian hope that place the light *only* at the end of the tunnel, that content themselves with inviting one to patience and endurance, when they do not incite one straight out to masochism by pushing one to seek suffering because it is "the sign of a privileged love of God." Is that all the meaning the Christian faith has to offer to life? And what should one do in the meantime while one is suffering and dying? Is the world of suffering opaque to such an extent that it rises up as an insurmountable obstacle before the life we confess? But in that case, perhaps it is necessary to ask, in effect, about the confession itself, so much does it seem to me un-Christian to see in the world and its limits (death included) only an obstacle to life.

So many things should be said about the harmful consequences that these customary visions entail in the lives of lay

181

A CHURCH OF THE BAPTIZED

people as well as in those of priests and bishops. With respect to
lay people, who does not see the cul-de-sac to which they are led
when it is claimed that the world constitutes their specific element? Can they experience *themselves* otherwise (since the world
defines them thus) than as an obstacle to true life, that which is
above? But I also wish to say how our understanding of the world
places clerics in a situation that some realize is untenable and
unbearable. By definition, they are outside the world.[10] How
could they not see themselves and not be considered by lay
people as *models* of Christian and ecclesiastical life? Since they
are accustomed to establishing themselves automatically at the
top, can they experience the world otherwise than as an obstacle?
But how could they not feel totally deprived when their own
experience teaches them that the world continues to define them
as well? For example, there are many who, after having learned
for a long time to understand themselves according to a sort of a-
temporal a-sexuality, find themselves powerless to manage their
sexuality as soon as the latter manifests a bit strongly its obstinate
right to existence. This house of straw then falls all the farther the
higher it had been set up by force.

To return explicitly to clergy/laity *relations*, it is evident that
the laity is condemned to play the killjoy in its relationships with
the clergy. This is easily seen in the tensions and the rejections
that clerical uniformity causes as soon as plurality is manifested.
Appointed as guarantors and guardians of unity, but of a unity
understood as uniformity, how will clerics welcome lay people as
soon as the latter manifest their right to personal and communal
differences?[11] Furthermore, how many lay people prefer to be
silent than to bring their originality into the church? Persons and
communities know too well the tensions created by their speaking
out, which they judge to be sterile tensions since clerics will
always know more and know better what is good and bad for the
church. This perverse mechanism is operative in parish and
diocesan life where priests and bishops do not cease to refer so

182

THE WORLD

easily and quickly to their privileged knowledge of what they call "the common good" in order to impose silence on goods that are definitely too individual and individualistic. But one notices more and more that Rome is entering into this game as soon as a particular church dares to manifest its own aspirations. It is so easy to appeal to a greater knowledge of the "universal" church in order to *generalize* and standardize the life of all the churches, even if the official discourses continue to affirm that each particular church is a realization of the universal church.

World and Guilt

The understanding of the world as an obstacle introduces the fifth trait, the final touch that characterizes the relations that Christians have learned to live with the world: *guilt-inducing* relations. I was led to speak of them as soon as it was a question of God, so much are our theistic visions the first invitation to nourish this guilt that I then called "pathological."[12] In fact, "the top," the entire top, clergy included, invites one to experience the world in the mode of guilt. In order to remain within reasonable limits, I shall refer here only to the so-called "official" sexual morality of the church in order to advance the four following points concerning the role of the clergy (and above all of the Roman authorities) in the construction and proposal of this moral discourse.

1. The Roman moral discourse has crystallized around several, not very numerous trouble spots that seem to obsess it like premarital relations, birth control, the situation of the divorced and remarried, and homosexuality. One could take up each one of these trouble spots again and show how the Roman discourse itself *creates* an unhealthy guilt (without wishing to, I hope). One only has to notice the results concerning homosexuality, for example. Perhaps the specialists in moral theology understand something of the position of Rome on homosexuality.[13] Unfortunately, not all homosexuals are specialists in moral

A CHURCH OF THE BAPTIZED

theology, and many seem to be totally crushed by the "official" declarations. For my part, I confess that they lose me. Affirming what is supposed to be an evident fact, a recent text first establishes as a principle that homosexuals are not sinners by the very fact that they are homosexuals, that their "inclination" is not itself a sin.[14] But I really do not see how one does not end up concretely in a negation of this principle when one presents homosexuality as a "tendency more or less strongly ordered to an intrinsic moral evil" and thus concludes that the inclination itself must be considered "as an objective disorder." Homosexuals are as torn in their lives between an inclination that is not sinful but becomes so as soon as it is acted upon as the mind is helpless before the understanding of human nature that this text conveys and the dichotomies the latter presupposes between being and acting, for example.[15]

2. I shall say soon why it is necessary that homosexuals, the divorced and remarried, and all those directly aimed at by the texts speak out. But I should first like to bring out a point that is essential to my purpose: beyond the words explicitly spoken by the authorities, it is urgently necessary to examine the presuppositions that are at work in the *construction* of these moral discourses. Behind each one, in effect, one notices a defect that is common to all: if each one is moralistic and guilt-inducing, and if they all are, it is because *the very way of "doing moral theology" is moralistic and guilt-inducing.*

One will have guessed the defect that, in my opinion, perverts the enterprise at its roots: the exclusively deductive movement I have been speaking of since the beginning of this book. It is, in effect, striking to notice how these discourses always appeal to the will of God or of Jesus Christ to furnish their own principles with an absolute validation and to justify the laws that will then be imposed on others. Do experts in scripture protest against the more than doubtful ways in which the authorities appropriate certain biblical texts for themselves? In the name of a "higher"

184

competency, the authorities (nevertheless) always find a way to resort to the texts to absolutize the rightness of their laws.

Furthermore, this mode of construction presupposes as well an opacity and a resistance of what is called the world, a sort of propensity that would be connatural to it to betray the will of God as soon as it is left to itself. [16] It makes such presuppositions even if it means advancing positions as tortuous for the understanding and as untenable from a Christian point of view as the following: "If one considers the world as it was at the beginning and as it should become again, it is self-evident that it is the creation of God, that it is good in itself, that we should love it as God himself has loved it, to the point of sacrificing ourselves for it. But if one considers the world as it has become as a result of sin, not at all the world as God willed it nor as he created it, but rather what we have made of it through our own fault, we have to recognize that the world has become the enemy of God and thus our enemy as well and that as such it must be overcome by this victory of which St. John still speaks and which is our faith."[17]

3. The *proposal* of the so-called "official" discourse equally causes a problem. Is there anything more frustrating than to hear it said and repeated until one cannot stand it anymore that these discourses are "the" discourse "of the church"? That is simply not true in the majority of cases. Is it true of one clerical authority, of certain Roman authorities in particular? Certainly. Of episcopal conferences? Often, but above all in those conferences that have confused collegiality and unanimity. Of all the priests and all the bishops? Evidently not. "Of the church," of the persons and communities to whom the declarations of principle have given the church? Absolutely not.

No one can deny the function of authority in the construction of the Christian moral discourse. But one would agree that authority will probably *serve* a liberating construction and proposal of the moral discourse the day it ceases to take itself as the church. [18] What else could one wish while waiting than that all

A CHURCH OF THE BAPTIZED

Christian persons and communities would take their responsibilities in order that a moral theology may be elaborated that would be faithful to the great imperatives of the good news? More precisely, will there ever be liberating words as long as the persons directly concerned do not enter into the construction and the proposal of the moral discourse of the church, as long as, for example, Christian homosexuals are held at a distance from the process that tries to express the Christian meaning of their homosexuality? The same question arises with respect to all the other particular points like birth control, the remarriage of divorced persons, etc. "The church" will probably not hold the same positions when its discernments are truly the work of the church and not only of the clergy, of those who have remained clerics.

4. It is necessary to notice that relations between clerics and lay people are booby-trapped and always bruise one or the other party, or both at the same time. It is useless to insist on this, since it should now be an evident fact. In the present organization of the church and, it must be made clear, when one is not acting by way of exception (when, for example, some "pastoral mercy" is not invoked that contradicts the absoluteness of the laws in practice), clerics are spontaneously perceived as moralizers who induce guilt, as censors of the world and of life. For their part, lay persons are constantly caught in the trap of relations that leave them torn apart, not because they have correctly realized their human limits there, but because the top invites them to live these limits *in the mode of guilt*. No one gains in truth and freedom there; all escape the work of this truth which, according to scripture, promises Christian freedom, and thus the freedom of relations to the world.

2. Lay People Are the Future of the Church

Faith in Jesus Christ demands a conversion of the images which we employ to shape our relations to God. At the same time this faith radically questions our spontaneous visions of the world and the relations to the world I have just described. Having reached the end of the course to which the structure of Christian mentality invites us, our reflection notices the challenges that *each* of the elements of the schema issues. Furthermore, however, it is *the coherence of the whole* that is challenged, the structure according to which the relationships between the different elements are organized. God was the point of departure, and all the rest flowed from this absolute beginning perceived as an absolute of beginning. To say clearly what I think (without, evidently, being able to enter into an explicit reflection on what is only affirmed), Christian faith confesses rather that in *Jesus Christ God and the world* are perfectly reconciled forever. Hence it follows that the first element of the Christian faith is not the God of our theistic schemas but our confession of Jesus Christ. The second element (at least in the order of the exposition) is the *encounter eternalized* at Easter of God and the world. One can see that the familiar schema is already deeply transformed and that, above all, a radically new dynamic has just appeared. Is that sufficient to suggest the enormous shift of the world, which is no longer situated last as an eminently passive object but enters into the confession of Jesus Christ?

All are invited here to a true conversion, a conversion on which the ecclesiastical future of the laity directly depends. At this last moment of the argument, what is at stake intensifies. It would be as well to state my case from the outset: not only do I believe that those who are called lay people *have* an ecclesiastical future; I also am certain of the fact that *they are the future of the church*. Perhaps the four following points will suffice to show that this statement is not empty and without content.

The World Is Necessary for Salvation

For too many people, the world is still perceived as an enemy to be combated, an obstacle to be overcome, if one no

A CHURCH OF THE BAPTIZED

longer wants to feel guilty about existing in this world. Bouyer said above: "If one considers the world as it has become as a result of sin, not at all the world as God willed it nor as he created it, but rather what we have made of it through our own fault, we have to recognize that the world has become the enemy of God and thus our enemy as well and that as such it must be overcome."[19] Let us have the humility to recognize that we do not know much about what God willed for the world in his eternity. Human pretensions are all the more perverse here as they emphasize the presumed perversity of the sole reality over which we have some control: *our* present world, this world that is said to be the enemy of God, no doubt in order better to erect it as *our* radical enemy. That being established, where else is the truth of the world to be sought if not "in the heart of God," i.e. at the top, a place that escapes the common condition of human beings, even though they be Christians? But is this not the very movement that Jesus Christ has converted? The Christian truth of the world, in the wake of Jesus and in the passage of his death and resurrection, must be sought *in* and *through* the world, if it is the case that the world, including death, was for Jesus Christ (and continues to be for us) a strictly necessary *condition* for *salvation* to be *possible* in history. Insofar as we are converted to Jesus Christ and the face of God that he reveals, the trajectory of our conversion to the world seems indeed to be from *enemy* to the *condition of possibility* for salvation and the things of faith (*res fidei*).

What is the demand that lay people then have to face? A long-standing habit pushes them to seek the salvation of the world everywhere except where the world, of itself, announces the challenges that individuals and collectivities have to take up. One is then amazed at the human insignificance of the Christian faith. Receiving the "enemy to be overcome" as their proper domain, will lay people exit from the void of their ecclesiastical status as long as the world is not read lovingly in its wedding with God himself in Jesus Christ?[20] I really look like an extra-terrestrial

188

THE WORLD

being when, in speaking of the church to married people, I ask them: When you "make love" (to use a familiar expression), is the church there, and does it change something in your human ways of "making love"?[21] Where should the church, Jesus Christ, and God himself be sought if not where the passover of Jesus Christ renders life in God and salvation *historically possible*, i.e. in the world? For my part, I notice that only those lay people find a certain ecclesiastical stability again who have dared to bring their faith home again in this way, who live a relationship to the world in which the latter is the (natural, so to speak) home of their (supernatural) faith.

I am certain that clerics are also summoned to a long and difficult process of conversion. They have learned so well to justify their type of mediation against the background of an estrangement from God, of his absence from the world.[22] Will they find their ecclesiastical identity again without a first conversion (not in a chronological) sense, quite evidently) that is their own conversion *to the world?* I believe that I know somewhat the existential stakes that charge this question. I shall point out only one of them that, in my opinion, is decisive: in order to find or to rediscover the ecclesiastical meaning of their service, priests and bishops must seek it in the world or, more precisely, in the *worldly condition of the church and in terms of it.*

The present authority of clerics rests upon their condition as subjects: established at the top, they are the true agent of clergy/laity relations. On the other hand, lay people have drifted toward the condition of a passive object because, when they enter into relationship with the clerics, they have nothing else than a world that, from the point of view of salvation, has come to fail in the place I have indicated. Is that not the type of relations that Jesus Christ comes to heal at its root? The mystery of his passover reveals, in effect, that he would not be mediator if his own humanity and his own worldliness had not intervened in the very act of mediation. For a church that claims to be truly of Jesus

189

A CHURCH OF THE BAPTIZED

Christ, the present structuring of clergy/laity relations is unjustifiable. This is not first of all because the ones *or* the others occupy a place that is unworthy of them. The reason for the rejection is much more fundamental: the relationships of Jesus Christ with the world forbid the very *relation* that presently *creates* clerics and lay people.[23]

The Christian Hope Concerning the World

Since the world thus constitutes a *condition of possibility* of Christian salvation, one cannot receive it in just any way. Faith demands a certain reading of the world, a reading that has to break with our customary pessimisms. It is simply not Christian to consider it merely as resistance, obstacle, or enemy to be overcome. No doubt, it must be worked and freed from its limits, so much do these limits render it fragile in the hands of individual and collective egoisms. But how, in that case, can it be worked if the prejudice at the outset is that it is not "workable"? How can it be transformed when it continues to be denied concretely and in fact (by our attitudes or by our actions) that it is transformable? In a word, it is not at all sufficient to confess it as a condition of possibility for a salvation that wishes to be history. It is further necessary to live, exist, and act in the world in a *hopeful* manner. And I shall add: in a manner that says that our Christian hope is also a hope *concerning* the world. Moltmann also brings out this character of Christian hope: "The God who calls and promises would not be God if he were not the God and the Lord of that reality into which his mission leads and if he could not create real and objective possibilities for his mission. The praxis of the transforming mission requires a certain world view, a trust and a hope concerning the world."[24] Let us understand that the very nature of God is in question here, so much is everything connected. Our God is not the god "of Jesus Christ," we do not live him, if, claiming to enroll ourselves in the transforming practice of Jesus, we approach the world as something that has to

190

THE WORLD

be got rid of in order to enter at last into God. The realism of the Christian faith confesses rather that, when persons and communities dedicate themselves lovingly to liberating the world, their world, they always set out in search of God.

Lay people are accustomed to receiving the truth of the world from the clergy. More generally, they have learned to read the world solely in terms of the top, in terms of God, Christ, the priests, the mass, and a church that prepossesses the truth of the world. Hence the measure of their task, an immense task that will never be finished as long as the world is world: they must also read each of the elements above *in terms of the world*. This is an essential dimension of hope. I am not preaching a magical vision of the world, a sort of naiveté that entrusts to the limits and to sin the concern to reveal, as limits and sin, the limitless and perfectly loving love of God in Jesus Christ. I am only saying that a liberating entry into the mystery of God, of Jesus Christ, and of the church is refused to anyone who absents himself or herself from limits and sin when he or she sets out to meet the Church, Jesus Christ, and God himself.

Consequently, the Christian hope concerning the world invites the clergy to difficult disappropriations. In fact, it demands them. I have often heard it said that, through the consistency and the insistence of their interference in the area of sexuality, clerics reveal that they are really sexually obsessed. No doubt, there are persons in their ranks, as everywhere else, who suffer from such obsessions. But that is not the essential point. Clericalism is fundamentally a malady *of authority*. I hope I have shown sufficiently that clerics are ill from a fallacious and (it is necessary to use the word) perverse power that gives a tranquil prepossession of the truth. What becomes of the clergy the moment lay people, in the name of their hope, assume responsibility for seeking the truth, of making it rise up from their own situation in the world? Can celibate clerics, for example, continue to interfere in the lives of couples so much (so awkwardly and

191

A CHURCH OF THE BAPTIZED

ponderously, one is inclined to say) when Christian hope affirms that the laws of this life are also discovered *in* the life of family and relations? The condition of "servant" may appear simple when texts on ordained ministry affirm it as a principle. The Christian hope concerning the world, however, lets one guess the ballast that will have to be discharged and, what is even more difficult, the decentering to be lived. The wager that ordained ministers are constantly invited to place again and again is that there is a promise of freedom in this enterprise of decentering when they renounce their little truths in order that the human truth of persons and communities may come about.

It would be simplistic to hold that Christian hope necessitates the conclusion that lay persons will become the subject of the church the day that clerics have become its object. There are reversals of steam that change the direction but finally end at the same destination. It is, however, evident that lay people do not affirm their ecclesiastical dignity and responsibility without the present structure of clergy/laity relationships being destroyed in the process. Led by the same hope concerning the world, everyone (including ordained ministers) is united in a common ecclesiastical mission that knows no top or bottom: sacramentalizing the liberating power of Easter in a world that has become capable, thanks to this same Easter, of writing a history that would be the history of salvation.

The Christian Love for the Autonomy of the World

The Christian hope does not reduce to a more or less pronounced tendency toward optimism. The latter is a question of hormones, nervous impulses, and physiological and psychological tone, whereas hope (in its principle: Jesus Christ) is not "more" alive among the optimists and "less" so among the pessimists. It does not vary according to the fluctuations of personal or collective psychology. It is nourished by this attitude: the world, the situation that the world creates for believers, is a condition

192

that must *always* be respected in order that salvation may be historically possible. As such, Christian hope is the exact opposite of a flight from the world or of a passive waiting for a beyond where real life will finally be lived. An analogy may be of service here: I am always already alive when I decide to give a meaning to my life. In a similar way, Christian faith confesses that the world is always already there when persons and communities dedicate themselves to transforming it. And, in order not to deny what was established previously, *it is always already there as a possibility of salvation.* Thus, *the Christian faith confesses the autonomy of the world* rather than denying it or holding it in contempt. Fully respecting the world when one searches for salvation there and fully respecting death when we seek life there—such is the road on which the work of Christian hope sets out untiringly. How can the world express salvation? How can death give life? One thing is certain: no answer is valid from a Christian point of view if it is formulated without a true love of the world (including death) *as* world.

I shall now return to the question of plurality raised in the preceding chapter in order to suggest at least what the autonomy of the world implies when lay people want to live there the church they believe. The uniformity of clericalism provides security in that it clearly delimits the "form" of each element above, all the way up to the definition of God. To give to the world its full place, to respect its autonomy, is first of all to recognize that *it is manifold.* This plurality is evident in long-term relations, in politics, for example, where differences of system produce different types of life in society. Plurality is perhaps even more disturbing when one realizes to what extent it is operative in each of us. In particular, no one can rest in what he or she was in order to define what he or she is and should become. Nevertheless, plurality is much more than a simply recorded fact. It *emerges from the act of faith itself* when persons and communities, responding to the urges of the same hope in universal communion, respect the

193

A CHURCH OF THE BAPTIZED

autonomy of the world, of their world, and of their own situation in the world. How, then, could they express their faith in the mode of uniformity and of identity? Communion thus becomes manifold, not contenting itself with tolerating differences, but demanding the emergence of originality. By taking the life of the church upon themselves, lay persons will thus have to learn at the same time that it does not exist in the world without tensions and conflicts, without the dispersion of individuals and collectivities ever ceasing to be a threat, a dispersion that would be opposite of the communion confessed.

If this is the case, it would be as well to say that clericalism answers to security needs that originate in the deepest part of each being. Lay people are always its victims, but it is understood that they can also be the best of its accomplices. By proposing uniformity, by defining themselves by the possession of the truth as it should be applied in the world, clerics simultaneously assure their power and momentarily reassure lay people by calming the fear of division that always risks taking possession of them, a fear of dying that is equally a fear of living. It is always easier to fall asleep in uniformity that to commit oneself to the building up of an ecclesiastical unity that will always be a process of genesis and will thus never be an established uniformity in which to repose. But what will happen to the clerics when lay people learn to risk their lives and to live their deaths? The clergy will lose the role of exorcist that it had given itself or that had been entrusted to it. The mission that it has granted itself of guaranteeing the unity of the church in the face of and against every threat of division thus becomes insignificant. *Clerics* lose everything there; *ordained ministers*, however, have everything to gain there. It will no doubt become possible for them, in effect, to discover their integration into the sacrament of the church: they constitute *one* particular sacrament *in the service* of a church that sacramentalizes Jesus Christ in and through his love for the world and the autonomy of the world.

194

Deciding the Future of God by Deciding the Future of the World

Everything that precedes does not mean that the believing condition has nothing to offer to the world. There is indeed a Christian confession that reveals a meaning. But it is literally a *confession*. It is borne by a certitude without this certitude being able to degenerate into a recipe, an answer possessed *before* there appear the world and, as a result, questions to which no one was accustomed. As such, the confession is irreducible to an answer fabricated by intelligence and applicable in every situation where the world is in question. It is irreducible to a human knowledge capable of answering thoroughly for its philosophy of the world. In one word as in a thousand, in words of the intellect but especially in words learned from real life, believers have to *seek* with all their brothers and sisters in humanity the meaning of freedom that should dwell in and transform the world. They are nevertheless sure that the God of Jesus Christ is waiting for them where the world is in the process of becoming and that the world is capable of giving life. That is the reason I should say their faith is essentially a question also. Their own truth as believers is elaborated in and through the worldly responses they give, often in darkness, to the calls of the world. Such is the fundamental reason that makes it understood that the certitude of faith is constantly being called to translate itself into *human decision*. In the name of their faith, persons and communities have to decide the *future of the world*, being sure that, in doing so, they are deciding the *future of God*.

Lay people know very well the innumerable decisions to which life invites them. Married or single life, the rearing of children, the responsibilities of a friendship, the managing of a budget, the conducting of political life, and even the choice between one macro-economic organization or another—everything calls for decision. The problem is the following: by exiling God and the things of the faith, the structure of ecclesiastical life has not taught them that, by thus deciding the future of the world, their

A CHURCH OF THE BAPTIZED

world, they are also deciding the future of God, if indeed the God of Jesus Christ is in question. As long as the organization prevents them from wedding love of God and love of the world in their decisions, this organization will favor disastrous dichotomies, psychologically alienating dichotomies in certain limit cases, but always favorable to schizophrenic patterns of behavior. Their decision in favor of God will continue to be made in a foreign universe, one other than this earth, elsewhere than in this world. The death and resurrection of Jesus Christ, that human decision in favor of God which is equally a decision of God in favor of the world, deserves that everyone become the *subject of God* where all become *subject of the world.* Can a more serious responsibility be imagined? At the same time, can a greater poverty of God be imagined, who eternally continues to wed his fate in history to always limited individual and collective decisions demanded by the present situation of the world?

At bottom, clericalism uses this poverty of God as a pretext for taking his place. The human decisions of clerics, called clericalism, *then become identical to the decisions of God.* The totalitarianism of the clergy is thus more serious than one is led to think: it is only rendered possible thanks to another totalitarianism that obstructs the future of God by blocking the future of the world. Conversely, one notices that where priests and bishops have renounced their domination they have truly served a freeing of personal and communal responsibility, a freeing that, for its part, has restored a future to worldly situations that were often near to despair. By persisting in their pre-defined answers, and especially by stubbornly giving themselves the power to tell the truth of the world *before* the appearances of the world, clerics are perhaps assuring themselves of a future and guaranteeing their ecclesiastical place for tomorrow and the day after. They are nevertheless losing the future of the ordained ministry. Why do persons and communities continue to receive priests and bishops, to give meaning to this particular sacrament, if the sole profit they draw from it is a mutilation of the life of the world and of their life today? Has not that life been visited in Jesus Christ by a love that always renders possible the liberation of the world? In spite of its claims to the contrary, clericalism is not life-giving, for nothing participates in the freedom of the Christian life that does not serve the liberation of the world.

"Does the laity have a future?" I have asked myself deep down all throughout this work. I should not have persisted in this work of reflection and of writing if I were without hope before this question. There are at least *five points* that I hope to have established sufficiently. They will close this book. I only hope that they will serve the openness of the church, its fidelity to Jesus Christ, and its love of God in his love for the world, that inviolable love that alone is able unceasingly to restore to it the beginnings of life. For this is what the church is called to: "To go from beginning to beginning through beginnings that have no end" (Gregory of Nyssa).

As defined by their present relationships with clerics, lay people have no future. This is the case for one primary, fundamental reason: *lay people have no future because they simply do not have an ecclesiastical present.*

The second point well expresses the shifting of the question to which I have wanted to invite the reader throughout this work: those who continue to be called "lay people" do not *have* an ecclesiastical future, they *are* the future of the church.

Such a statement, however, is in no way a facile concession to the tastes of the day, nor is it condescendence that is as contemptuous as it is apparently generous. It rather expresses the responsibility that would be untenable without the memory of the active presence of the Lord. In effect, my third point states that *the church and its future belong to all those who, wedding the future of God with the future of the world in their decisions, truly assume their status as subject of life in the church.*

197

A CHURCH OF THE BAPTIZED

Priests and bishops have also been baptized into this reality. In order to forsake clericalism, they must necessarily *reintegrate this common condition* outside which nothing has any Christian meaning and with respect to which everything is only service.

Hence my fifth and last point: *the laity of today has no Christian meaning* insofar as it is made to exist by clerical structures that insult the mystery of Jesus Christ. In order to last, these structures demand a bill that cannot and should not be paid: the passivity of lay people. In a church of faith in Jesus Christ, there can no longer be a subject and an object of ecclesiastical life. There are no longer any clerics or lay people.

Notes

Chapter 1

1. For a pertinent collection of more properly theological testimonies, analyses, and reflections, I refer the reader to the collection of Michel-M. Campbell and Guy Lapointe, eds., *Relations clercs/laïcs. Analyse d'une crise*, Cahiers d'études pastorales, no. 1 (Montréal: Fides, 1985).

2. I add that if the Roman authorities have finally taken up the question of the laity again and are proposing it to the upcoming synod, it is because it is being posed throughout the Catholic world and is raising henceforth ineluctable challenges.

3. This is the first question that one must pose to *Vocation and Mission of the Laity in the Church and in the World Twenty Years after the Second Vatican Council*, the *Lineamenta* from Rome for the preparation of the upcoming synod. Henceforth, when I refer to this text, I shall designate it simply as *Lineamenta*, and I shall cite the United States Catholic Conference edition.

4. The continuation of my reflections will show why I gladly take up this definition of B. Sesboué: "The term 'structure' evokes with greater rigor (than 'idea' or 'essence') in the recent researches of mathematics and the human sciences *an organic totality of elements that maintain among themselves a play of relations such that the displacement or modification of the one inevitably entails the displacement or modification of others.* . . . The coherence and intelligibility (of the structure) are thus always to be sought within the framework of its total unity. Likewise, if an element is taken for the whole, or if, conversely, it ceases to function, the structure collapses" ("Ministères et structures de l'Église," *Le ministère et les ministères dans le Nouveau Testament*, Parole de Dieu [Paris: Seuil, 1974], 349; the italics are mine).

A CHURCH OF THE BAPTIZED

5. Once again I agree with B. Sesboué. Although he makes clear that he is working on the "structures," he no less seeks to aim at the "mystery" of the church. And he adds that his study "is thus situated at the level of fundamental ecclesiology, which does not mean that it treats an abstract question without any impact on the present and future lives of ecclesiastical communities" (ibid.).

6. "We have passed from a world of objects to a world of the subject. It would be stupid to accuse the fathers and the great scholastics of not having recognized the originality of the person. St. Thomas says that it represents the highest form of being. But the grandiose meditation where he says this (C. Gent. IV, 11) is particularly typical of the ancient and medieval fashion of approaching things. *It consisted in situating them in the great hierarchical chain of beings and, within this ordered succession, in interpreting them in terms of ontology. Thus the free person and the ethical order appeared as objectively normed by an order posited by God, the creator and legislator*" (Y. Congar, *Ministères et communion ecclésiale* [Paris: Cerf, 1971], 236; the italics are mine).

7. Cited by Yves Congar, *L'Église de saint Augustin à l'époque moderne*, Histoire des dogmes, no. 20 (Paris: Cerf, 1970), 457.

8. R. Rémond, cited in P. Guilmot, *Fin d'une Église cléricale?* Histoire des doctrines ecclésiologiques (Paris: Cerf, 1969), 9.

9. For its part, the text of the *Lineamenta* is woven together of conciliar citations. But through its ignorance of the conciliar dynamics, it marks a clear retreat with respect to the great movements that bore the reflection of Vatican II, as I shall soon have occasion to show.

10. These words of P. Glorieux testify to this: "These latter alone (the 'legitimate heads' of the church) have the authority to make the decisions that they judge to be fitting and to make them binding in conscience. Others may propose, attempt to convince, enlist support. But they have the right to bind in the name of Christ whom they represent and continue" (*Le laïc dans l'Église* [Paris: Éditions Ouvrières, 1960], 207). Hence the invitation issued to lay people to take their place "in the ranks": "remaining in his or her place in the ranks, the lay person instinctively finds the attitude expected of him or her vis-à-vis the hierarchy, even if Catholic Action has made it reach a higher level of responsibility" (ibid., 205).

NOTES

11. A judgment that A. Charron seems to share, for whom the categories "clergy" and "laity" "are correlative, and the one should disappear with the other." He thus proposes that these categories be "surpassed" and even "suppressed" ("Surpass the categories 'clergy' and 'laity' and restore the mission of Christians in the church and in the world" is to appear in the "Actes du Congrès de 1986 de la Société canadienne de théologie").What I have just said will at least let one guess why the *Lineamenta* seem to me to be of such a great (and sad) poverty and why I do not think that one can expect much of the upcoming synod if it works in the spirit of this text. The *Lineamenta* speak extensively of the laity, very rapidly of the ordained ministries, *but never broach the question of the present structure of their relations.* This document is thus interested in everything but that which constitutes "real life." One can already foresee a final declaration animated by good feelings toward lay people and no doubt warm in its exhortations but, as other texts produced by certain prior synods, without real weight on the concrete conduct of the ecclesiastical organization.

12. Art. "Église," IV:2114.

13. I did not think it good, in particular, to take up the historical surveys that have been so well done elsewhere and to review the results, which one will easily find in the numerous recent writings on the laity. But I would regret not recommending the reading of the excellent book of A. Faivre, *Les laïcs aux origines de l'Église*, Chrétiens dans l'histoire (Paris: Le Centurion, 1984).

Chapter 2

1. *La théologie contemporaine (1945–1980)* (Paris: Le Centurion, 1982), 315. The italics are mine. H.P. Owen specifies: "Theism signifies belief in one God (*theos*) who is (a) personal, (b) worthy of adoration, and (c) separate from the world but (d) continuously active in it" (art. "Theism," in *The Encyclopedia of Philosophy* (1967), VIII:97). That is why "theism always involves the belief that God is continuously active in the world. In this it differs from deism. According to deism . . . God, having made the world at the beginning of time, left it to continue on its own. Theism (notably Aquinas), on the other hand, maintains that every item in the world depends for its existence on the continuous activity of God as the creator" (ibid., col. 98).

A CHURCH OF THE BAPTIZED

2. "But being preceded by these words of God, the moment arrives when we ask ourselves: Is it truly possible to believe? In this sense, *doubt is found at the heart of all believers*. Unamuno said: A *faith that does not doubt is a dead faith*"—A. Dumas, *Ces mots qui font croire et douter* (Paris: Éditions Oecuméniques, 1971), 29. The italics are mine.

3. J.-C. Sagne, "Du besoin à la demande, ou la conversion du désir dans la prière," *Pax* 167 (June 1973):11.

4. Op. cit., 337.

5. G. Brassens, in "Toute une vie pour la chanson. André Sève interroge Georges Brassens," *Les interviews* (Paris: Le Centurion, 1975), 119–120.

6. *Women* (Santa Barbara: Black Sparrow Press, 1979), 177.

7. Excerpted from *Traité des saints Ordres*, cited by R. Salaün and É. Marcus, *Qu'est-ce qu'un prêtre?* (Paris: Seuil, 1965), 33.

8. No. 22.

9. This text from no. 9 of *Presbyterorum Ordinis* is taken up by the *Lineamenta*, no. 7.

10. "Les laïcs en 1980," *Relations* 458 (April 1980):114.

11. Ibid., 115.

12. "Theism does not deal with such central Christian doctrines as the Incarnation and the Atonement, and because its teaching about God is not tied to christology, some theologians question whether its God is the same as the one whom Christians know in faith as the God and Father of Jesus Christ" (T. Early, art. "Theism," *Encyclopedic Dictionary of Religion* [1977], III:3488).

13. *Libérer Jésus* (Paris: Le Centurion, 1977), 38.

14. "The lay person will help the priest to be truly a priest by his eagerness to receive the priestly gift, influence, doctrine, sacraments, and laws of the gospel—all these things being laden with grace. Through his testimony of the Christian life in the world, the lay person will pursue in all lateral directions the *descending movement issuing from God*"—G. Philips, *Le rôle du laïcat dans l'Église* (Tournai and Paris: Casterman, 1954), 151. The italics are mine. The ecclesiological logic of this text is clear. An entirely different logic is proposed in a short but very interesting article by G. Raymond ("Le rôle des fidèles dans la

NOTES

manifestation, la reconnaissance et la proclamation de la Révélation") which appeared in the *Actes du Congrès de 1986 de la Société canadienne de théologie*.

Chapter 3

1. *Jésus Christ à l'image des hommes* (Paris: DDB, 1978), 21.

2. *Jésus de Nazareth, histoire de Dieu, Dieu de l'histoire* (Paris: Cerf, 1984), 184–185.

3. Ibid.

4. One will read his recently re-edited major work with profit: *La résurrection de Jésus mystère de salut* (Paris: Cerf, 1982). Cf. also *L'Eucharistie, sacrement pascal* (Paris: Cerf, 1980).

5. *Le bouclier d'Athéna. L'Occident, son histoire et son destin* (Paris: Robert Laffont, 1983), 106.

6. One understands that the vast majority of believers continue to be fashioned by such schemas of thought when one realizes that christology itself, in the judgment of B. Sesboué, hardly begins to react against such a vision and such designs: "In reaction against a theology that was too immediately entangled in the analysis of the divinity of Jesus and running the risk of undermining the reality and the conditions of his human existence, christology today takes its point of departure from his humanity. It is there that it wishes to read first the expression of the filial relation of Jesus to his Father, which is constitutive of his identity"— *Jésus Christ dans le temps de l'Église* (Paris: Desclée, 1982), 38.

7. *La théologie contemporaine (1945–1980)* (Paris: Le Centurion, 1982), 359–360.

8. One will permit me to refer here to the first chapter of my book *Condition chrétienne et service de l'homme. Essai d'anthropologie chrétienne*, Héritage et Projet, no. 4 (Paris: Cerf, 1973), Cogitatio Fidei, no. 74 (Montréal: Fides, 1973), 21–60. I there reproduce the text of *Document IV*. The entire first chapter of this book is, moreover, dedicated to the evolution of conciliar thought concerning the relationships between the baptismal priesthood and the ordained ministry.

9. "In referring to these words of our Master which contain the most marvelous *wishes* for the anniversary of our priesthood . . ." (*Lettre du pape Jean-Paul II à tous les prêtres de l'Église à l'occasion du*

A CHURCH OF THE BAPTIZED

Jeudi-Saint 1985, typographie polyglotte vaticane, no. 3). To me this perspective seems rather foreign to Vatican II. For my part, I do not see how the conciliar texts could justify celebrating Holy Thursday as the "anniversary" of the "priesthood" of priests and bishops.

10. P.-E. Bonnard and P. Grelot, art. "Messie," *Vocabulaire de théologie biblique*, 3rd ed. (Paris: Cerf, 1971), col. 752.

11. The *Lineamenta* maintain, for example, that this is what constitutes its "typical ecclesial condition" (no. 23).

12. *Der gekreuzigte Gott. Das Kreuz Christi als Grund und Kritik christlicher Theologie* (Munich: Chr. Kaiser Verlag, 1972), 200.

13. Ibid., 201.

14. *Beauté du monde et souffrance des hommes* (Paris: Le Centurion, 1980), 175. The italics are mine.

15. Ibid., 303.

Chapter 4

1. Henri Denis, "La théologie du presbytérat de Trente à Vatican II," in *Les prêtres. Formation, ministère et vie*, Unam Sanctam, no. 68 (Paris: Cerf, 1968), 209.

2. K. Rahner and H. Vorgrimler, *Kleines Theologisches Wörterbuch*, 14th ed. (Freiburg: Herderbücherei, 1983), 279.

3. "Le sacerdoce du Nouveau Testament," in *Les prêtres. Formation, ministère et vie*, 238.

4. Let us note in passing "the refusal of Vatican II to take the title *alter Christus* into consideration for priests"—Hervé Legrand, "Le développement d'Églises-sujets, une requête de Vatican II," in *Les Églises après Vatican II. Dynamisme et perspective*, Actes du colloque international de Bologne—1980, ed. by G. Alberigo, Théologie historique, no. 61 (Paris: Beauchesne, 1981, 171).

5. Introductory note to *Prêtre et Pasteur*, 83/2 (February 1980).

6. Hence the diagnosis I made, which holds for the church of Quebec but, no doubt, equally for many other churches (if not all), in "L'Église de Québec: une Église en mal de sujet," *Critère* 31 (Spring 1981):191–222.

7. Yves Jolif, "Notes philosophiques sur la médiation," in *Le ministère sacerdotal. Un dossier théologique* (Lyon: Profac, 1970), 219.

8. "If the insistence on the priesthood of Christ is not great in the New Testament, the affirmation of the unicity of his priesthood is, on the other hand, clear. Since no sacrifice can be added to his, since he is the present unique mediator between God and men, the priesthood falls, strictly speaking, to Christ alone"—H. Legrand, "Les ministères de l'Église locale," in *Initiation à la pratique de la théologie* (Paris: Cerf, 1983), III:220.

9. Y. Jolif, loc. cit., 219–220.

10. Pierre Grelot, *Église et ministères. Pour un dialogue critique avec Edward Schillebeeckx* (Paris: Cerf, 1983).

11. Ibid., 55.

12. Ibid., 73.

13. Ibid., 180.

14. Ibid., 133.

15. Ibid., 133–134.

16. Ibid., 180. The theme of "prolongation" returns often in Grelot's book.

17. "La compréhension dogmatique du service sacerdotal," *Concilium* 43 (n.d.):25.

18. Grelot, *Église et ministères*, 38.

19. Ibid., 142.

20. Ibid., 194.

21. H. Denis, "La théologie du presbytérat de Trente à Vatican II," 209. I have put the negation in italics.

22. This judgment is corroborated by the authors of *Situation et avenir du catholicisme québécois. Entre le temple et l'exil* (Montréal: Leméac, 1982): "Since that time (i.e., the first half of the twentieth century), one has certainly spoken of the church as the people of God and of the importance of the role of lay people. But studies made in the course of recent years teach us that lay people still identify the church and the hierarchy" (p. 223).

23. "The majority of believers do not have the chance to appropriate the reality of the church. If, for the ones, the church appears to hold the place of the religious authority in everything and to dispense them from feeling responsible, for others it seems more and more to be an addition, a mediation, and sometimes even a screen which is often

A CHURCH OF THE BAPTIZED

difficult to bear. *The integration of the ecclesiastical dimension in the attitude of faith has not been adequately made*" (ibid., 254). The italics are mine.

24. This is the reason that the *Lineamenta* effect, in my opinion, a return to the period before Vatican II. They do not pose the question of the laity *in its relations* to the clergy and thus do not give an account of the problems as they are concretely experienced. But, at the same time, they also refuse in just as concrete a manner to understand the invitation the council addresses to us to convert our customary ways of living and thinking of the church by making all the subject of the church.

25. W. Kaspar, art. cit., 26.

26. P. Grelot, *Le ministère de la nouvelle alliance*, Foi vivante, no. 37 (Paris: Cerf, 1967), 119. I do not see how, in the logic of the anthropological foundations sketched here, Grelot can still hold to the discourse on the ordained ministry analyzed above.

27. The expression comes from H. de Lubac, *Méditation sur l'Église*, Foi Vivante, no. 60 (Paris: Aubier, 1968), 104.

28. The people of God "is in no way comprised of groups of the faithful entrusted to pastors, but of the entire community to which both clerics and lay people belong. Priests and bishops are members of this people as baptized persons and as ministers. They are not ahead or above the people but within it"—N. Provencher, "Vers une église totale," *Église et théologie* 15/1 (1984):85–86.

29. H. Legrand is thus right in criticizing "the present system of access to the presbyteral ministry." This system "is that of the candidacy of generally young volunteers accepting celibacy. This voluntary service, which corresponds psychologically to an inner call, is called 'vocation' in ordinary language and even in more or less official texts." After having shown how "two innovations of the Codex of 1983 accentuate this subjectivity of vocation even more," he reminds us that such a view "cannot purely and simply appeal to the tradition" ("Les ministères de l'Église locale," 246).

Chapter 5

1. "The Ministry and Life of Priests," no. 2.

2. *Fin d'une Église cléricale?* (Paris: Cerf, 1969), 345.

NOTES

3. Recall the expressions reported by Y. Congar that I cited in the preceding chapter.

4. Cf. Chapter Two.

5. "Mystery and Worship of the Holy Eucharist," *Origins* 9/41 (1980):663. The italics are mine.

6. Among the questions posed to sacramental theology today, R. Didier recalls the fact that the church "seems to delight in an *ex opere operato* theology where attention focused almost exclusively on the efficaciousness of gestures borders on magic"—*Les sacrements de la foi. La Pâque dans ses signes*, Croire et comprendre (Paris: Le Centurion, 1975), 16.

7. Henri Denis, *Les sacrements ont-ils un avenir?* (Paris: Cerf, 1971), 82.

8. I use the quotation marks in order to remind the reader that it is a question of a sign as it is understood in the logic that has been analyzed, i.e. in the sense of a physical causality that reifies and objectifies.

9. If it is true that Christian faith, hope, and charity do not annul the human responsibility to decide the meaning of our lives, is it not necessary to speak of a *submission* of the sacrament to the decision of believers? "In order to avoid sacramentalism," writes R. Didier, "it will first be necessary to show that the sacrament is submitted to faith, hope, and charity. Only then will we be able to affirm that it is *necessary* for them" (op. cit., 110). I thus do not deny the proper efficacy of the sacraments. I am only saying that, in order to be Christian, this efficacy in one way or another demands the intervention of the human decision of believers. Once this demand has been met, one will rediscover to what extent the eucharist and the other sacraments are in effect *necessary* to the existence of faith, hope, and charity.

Chapter 6

1. Lalande, *Vocabulaire technique et critique de la philosophie*, 10th ed. (PUF, 1968), 1160.

2. "Le christianisme est-il une idéologie?" *Concilium* 6 (1965):41 and 61.

3. Ibid., 42.

4. This sort of naiveté makes one fear the institutional regress that

the church is undergoing all the more. With respect to episcopal collegiality, for example: ". . . apart from the ecumenical or general council, the exercise of collegial responsibility in the service of the universal communion of the churches is poor in institutional occasions to the point of appearing visibly atrophied. On the one hand, this atrophy explains the vague or very generic formulation of Vatican II, but, on the other, it exposes one of the principal causes of the difficulty and the slowness with which the church seeks to respond to the demands to share responsibility"—G. Alberigo, "Institutions exprimant la collégialité entre l'épiscopat universel et l'évêque de Rome," in *Les Églises après Vatican II. Dynamisme et prospective* (Paris: Beauchesne, 1981), 271.

5. D. Sesboué and J. Guillet, art. "Communion," *Vocabulaire de théologie biblique* (Paris: Cerf, 1970), 189.

6. It would, in effect, be necessary to question at length the perception that is generally had of eternity and of its relationships with human time. A Christian category as important as that of the *kingdom*, for example, suffers the harmful consequences of these poorly considered relationships.

7. Jean Duché, *Le bouclier d'Athéna. L'occident, son histoire et son destin* (Paris: Robert Laffont, 1983), 168.

8. Ibid., no. 11.

9. J.-M. Levasseur, "La spécificité du presbytérat," in *Le prêtre, hier, aujourd'hui, demain* (Montréal: Fides, 1970), 371–372. Cardinal Doepfner says nothing different: ". . . this priesthood of all the faithful finds in the ministerial priesthood its central point, its recapitulation, its sacramental expression"—"Le prêtre: ce qui demeure, ce qui change," *Documentation Catholique* 66 (1960):174.

10. "To the laity in particular," the *Lineamenta* affirms, "falls the task of the Christian animation of the temporal order" (no. 30).

11. Cited in the *Lineamenta*, no. 24.

12. Ibid., no. 9.

13. This was said at the Olympic Stadium in Montreal during the visit of John Paul II to Canada in 1984. This cry seems, moreover, to have caused such a surprise that it made the newspaper headlines.

14. *Ministères et communion ecclésiale* (Paris: Cerf, 1972), 246.

NOTES

15. For a clarification of a problematic hardly sketched here, one will permit me to refer to my book *Communion et pluralité dans l'Église. Pour une pratique de l'unité ecclesiale*, Héritage et Projet, no. 24 (Montréal: Fides; Paris: Le Centurion, 1980).

16. In the text of *The Ministry and Life of Priests* that I cited above, one should, in effect, note the employment of the accusative *"in unum corpus."*

Chapter 7

1. I wish to note first of all that "the world" is a notion with a very hazy conceptual content. For my part, I think that at the root of the defect from which our understandings suffer there is above all a really simplistic objectivation. It would be necessary rather to think of the world as "a *mixture* in which man is no longer separable from the earthly milieu that conditions him while being molded by him"—J.-M. Aubert, *Pour une théologie de l'âge industriel*, Cogitatio Fidei, no. 59 (Paris: Cerf, 1971), 287. For the purpose of this chapter, I shall recall that "Christianity and above all the gospel of John" have given a new meaning to the concept: "the world is the ensemble of creatures as opposed to the creator, and more precisely, that which in this suddenly degraded cosmos (still ignorant of the fact) most distances man from spiritual demands: the wisdom of the world is opposed to the foolishness of the cross, whereas it is the latter that saves. One can be tempted by the glory of the world, but it is the nature of such a glory to pass away. . . . Hence the theme of separatism which has gathered momentum from the beginnings of Christian thought"—P.-F. Moreau, *La philosophie* (Paris: CEPL, 1977), 348. A "separatism" that defines the world "in opposition to the creator" is no doubt what Christian life and reflection are invited to convert today.

2. Cited previously in Chapter Four.

3. Oechslin writes, for example, that lay people "are the immense vanguard of the church. They bear the responsibility for its growth in the world." But the immensity of their mission is strictly controlled by the clerics of whom I spoke in the fourth chapter: the lay person, in effect, "while forging ahead in the world, remains tied to the truth and to the source of life through his fidelity to the

209

A CHURCH OF THE BAPTIZED

leaders of the church"—*Une spiritualité des laïcs* (Paris, 1963), 190 and 191.

4. Here is an illustration of this movement of church/world relationships: "After a long tradition of protest against the modern world, then of isolation, the church of the twentieth century has effected a true metanoia in its attitude toward the world since the last war and especially since Vatican II. It was a multiform conversion in its manifestations. From the mistrustful church that it was, it has become accessible and welcoming. . . . Before, it pretended to give without receiving, to know all without having to learn. Today, it recognizes that it receives and that it learns much from the world. It recognizes the world as a free partner in an open dialogue"—R. Latourelle, *Le Christ et l'Église, signes du salut* (Montréal: Bellarmin, 1971), 178.

5. It should be evident that I am not inviting one here to an absorption of the world by the church. But one will at least agree from the fact that, to take up again the expressions of Paul VI, the economy, politics, culture, etc. are also operative in the interior of the church. This recognition seems to me a capital one. One often hears it said that the clergy and the laity should be redefined in terms of a common *mission* of the church in the world. That is all well and good, but on the condition that the presence of the world in the church first be perceived.

6. Where will lay people be in the upcoming synod that will deal with them? More precisely, after having been widely consulted in certain churches, what will become of them at the moment decisions are made *about* them and *about* their lives?

7. One will note the passage from the plural (lay people) to the singular (the subject). This passage is explicitly deliberate. It indicates at least this much: it is the *communal* dimension of each one that makes all to be the church (in the singular).

8. Hence the still common conceptions of religious *practice*: "Formerly, religious 'practice' was situated on the margins of daily life. It was a thing that was experienced only at church or at home at one moment of prayer or another. . . . The world was often simply considered as a trampoline for lifting oneself to a higher region where it became possible to praise God and to practice virtue. Its proper meaning was not perceived. Interest in the problem of earthly existence seemed to

be exclusively reserved for those who claimed to be unbelievers"—E. Schillebeeckx, *Le monde et l'Église. Approches théologiques* (Bruxelles: Cep, 1967), 150–151.

9. "Signification ecclésiale du laicat," *Lumière et Vie* 65 (November–December 1963):86.

10. Cf. the citation I commented on in Chapter One.

11. Cf. the preceding chapter.

12. Cf. above, Chapter One.

13. Even if one can doubt it when one sees the fate being meted out to the American moralist Charles Curran.

14. Signed by Cardinal Ratzinger and made public October 31, 1986.

15. This is precisely a task that C. Curran proposes to moral theology: "Moral theology has also tried to overcome the older dichotomy between the supernatural and the natural, the gospel and daily life, and the church and the world. All the dichotomies basically come from the same two-layer view of the world no longer accepted by most contemporary Catholic moral theologians. The natural order as such does not exist and never has existed. There is only one history. The gospel and God's loving gift must be related to the personal, political, social and economic circumstances in which we live"—*Transition and Tradition in Moral Theology* (Notre Dame: University of Notre Dame Press, 1979), 4.

16. Hence the *suspicion* which I said earlier weighs on lay people: "One can understand that the ethical question is where the shoe pinches believers the most when one remembers that the moral theology of the church makes a suspicion of arbitrariness, of subjectivism, weigh upon the judgment of conscience of the adult Christian, even in the domains where the defining cleric has no experience"—J. Grand'Maison, "Une vocation originale pour les laïcs d'ici," in *Situation et avenir du catholicisme québécois. Entre le temple et l'exil* (Montréal: Leméac, 1982), 182.

17. Louis Bouyer, *Introduction à la vie spirituelle* (Paris: Desclée, 1960), 189.

18. With respect to the "official" moral discourse of the church, the moralist J.-G. Nadeau notes: "There is thus in this moral theology a

A CHURCH OF THE BAPTIZED

dichotomy of actors (we/they) and of the real (good/evil), a univocity of communication (from those who know to those who are ignorant, from clerics to lay people), and crowning the whole, the divine guarantee of the priestly or clerical discourse"—"Morale cléricale—morale laïque. Le rapport avec l'expérience dans leur discours et leur élaboration," in M.-M. Campbell and G. Lapointe, eds., *Relations clercs-laïcs. Analyse d'une crise*, Cahiers d'études pastorales, no. 1 (Montréal: Fides, 1985), 238.

19. Cf. note 17 of this chapter.

20. An appeal is thus issued that T. Rast also hears: "Contempt for the reality of the world placed under the sign of a futuristic eschatological Christianity has not only been here and there the forte of ascetics and even more of the theoreticians of asceticism but also the temptation of the theologians"—"L'eschatologie," in *Bilan de la théologie du XXe siècle* (Casterman, 1970), 514.

21. It should be evident that I do not understand this presence of the church as the intrusion of a more or less inquisitorial moral theology. I am speaking here of the church that married people *are* and ought to *become*.

22. In the last analysis, this is what justified, in effect, the type of reified mediation analyzed in the fourth chapter.

23. The christological coherence that unifies both the numerous questions and the paths that open up manufactured "answers" is thus verified once more: "Thus, this schema organized by 'the top' (i.e. the classical model) treated the humanity of Jesus according to a logical reasoning that did not take account of the complexity of scripture: it was established, for example, that in virtue of his two natures Jesus possesses a consciousness that was humanly limited but illuminated as a result of his divinity, excluding every kind of ignorance and doubt and even including 'the beatific vision,'" whereas the gospels do not hesitate to speak of the ignorance of Jesus and of his faith. . . . Thus the critiques of this *descending* christology, especially since Pannenberg, are able to show that these theses were not only opposed to scripture in that they underestimated the humanity of Jesus but also that they assumed at the departure what had to be proved, namely, the divinity of Jesus"—B.

Lauret, "Christologie dogmatique," in *Initiation à la pratique de la théologie* (Paris: Cerf, 1982), II:268.

24. *Theologie der Hoffnung. Untersuchungen zur Begründung und zu den Konsequenzen einer christlichen Eschatologie*, Beiträge zur evangelischen Theologie, no. 38 (Munich, Chr. Kaiser Verlag, 1966), 266.